Chapter One

Christianity and Rejection

People always ask me if I am not tired of people insulting me each time I wrote an article. I tell them I am not. Perhaps I should narrate part of my early Christian. Most of my friends ran away, and I remember when I am passing people hide to call me names like Holy Spirit. I mean, I had never been called such names and funny ones until that age. When a mother found their child walking with me, they will beat them up. They will ask the child why he or she was walking with me and if he or she wanted to be "useless like that idiot" (that's me). Even classmates who could not even write a sentence both in our first, second or third languages would tell me I am stupid. They made fun of me as I went out and derided me as I came back.

Giving your life to Christ brought you shiners more than what criminals had. My in-law used to tell me: "you are the most wicked person going to church. You will not help your family if you become a Christian, and you will be useless. How many white people have you seen in church here"? As I look at it now, I laugh. We were living in a town with very few white people. So how was he going to see white people in church where there were no TV or the only one we had showed only the effigy of the president morning and night?

I remember one day how I visited one young man who gave his life to Christ. His father was a medical doctor. So he asked me for my name, parents and education. Then when I told him I had a degree, he said, "come in" and we began discussing about Christ. I was really too good for him. So he called the children and said: "this is the type of person you should listen to not these frustrated people out there who do not go to school". Christianity in those days was like taking money to buy shame.

As time went on, things began to change. One woman came to me one day and said: "I heard your father has died, yet you have kept yourself in school. Please, I want to give you my boy, so you could proselyte him." Soon many parents were calling me as the example in the quarter. I remember a nurse who used to work for Brasserie Du Cameroun who invited me to his house to teach his kids what a model child should be. I used to carry cooking pots, food and things on my head to go to the market with my mother when kids who were just in secondary school felt it was a shame. When the truck pusher who had to carry my mother's food to the market was delaying, I will carry part of it on my head, and my mother will carry the rest. It was a testament to the people in the quarters. Rather than everyone scorning at me the younger people mocked me, but their parents gave me the respect and wanted all their children to behave like me.

Christianity is more than just going to church my friends. It is more than just singing and talking about God. It is a lifestyle. That is what made my family to believe in Christ. They saw their kin change from a rascal to a gentleman.

Nonetheless, there were times I cried when people mocked me too much. I have cried too much when I was a young Christian that today I am a shame-proof. No matter how people mock me, I just laugh. Little kids will stand by the roadside; singing and clapping a mockery song. There were those who shot little stones and hid themselves. Wow! What rejection have I not seen? My body even itches if I do not hear people say those things again. Yeah, they instead make me laugh, and they now sound funny.

Sometimes I have fought back like when I was preaching in "Parlement" at Ngoa Ekelle, and a girl was disrupting my homily calling me, "frustration papa." She will ululate and say "frustration papa". So I stopped preaching because she was perturbing others from listening and gave her, her own medicine. I said: "look at you; you do not even have the name of a woman on your face. Will you too go if they wanted women to come to the presidency?" The crowd shouted, "woooohhhhhh." What I meant was that she was an ugly woman. She went quiet but moved closer to me. Methought she wanted to hear more about God. As I came closer, she landed me a dirty slap. My ears rumbled, and my eyes saw stars. From nowhere, a young man : not even in my group came and held her, pulled her by the side and began whooping her as if to kill a snake until I had to personally go and plead with the young man to leave her alone.

Today, almost everyone wants to be a Christian. This is wonderful. Rather than carry my bible secretly, I now write everywhere telling people I am a Christian. Wow! Lord I thank you for what you did for me and my friends. I look at most of them, they are still here. I wonder if I had not experienced rejection as a young man what would have happened to me these days with all the rejections one faces almost daily. Wow! God is really good! The good thing about my Christianity is that people have known me since when I was a child, and they do testify about my transformation. What else can a man want in life if it is not believing and serving Jesus Christ the only way of salvation?

Until then, be proud of your Christianity.

Chapter Two
Do You Need A Little More Push?

Is life stinging you like a bee? Are your kids sending you to a psychiatric ward? Have you lost your job, or is cancer tearing a relative apart? Is the devil roaring like a lion seeking to devour you? Know that after every winter comes spring. Resist the devil in prayers and he will flee away from you.

We all know that most of us do not like severe winter. The other day I read the story of the boll weevils. They cannot survive in severe winter and so cannot eat the crops of farmers. To those farmers, winter is a blessing. Please, turn your trials and temptations into blessings. Not every calamity is a curse; some are rather blessings and that can only happen through prayers. Are you praying enough? If your problems are overweighing you down then you have prayed less. If you pray enough, though you may still have the problems but you will have the peace and succor to bear the outcome. So are you praying enough? When was the last time you set a prayer time and place? When was the last time you prayed as if your life was on the line?

People say prayer renders a society backwards. Are all Muslim countries backward? Muslims do not pray for more than 30 minutes per session but did you know that each Muslim makes a total of 17 prayer rounds during the 5 daily prayers? The Morning Prayer has 2 prayer rounds, Noontime Prayer: 4 prayer rounds, Mid Afternoon prayer: 4 prayer rounds, Sunset prayer: 3 prayer rounds, and the evening prayer: 4 prayer rounds; making a total of 17 prayer rounds.

Paul urged believers to "pray without ceasing" (I Thes 5:17). Like the Praying Mantis, be in a praying position in your heart and acts. The phrase "praying always" (Lk

21:36; Eph 6:18; Col 1:3) simply means communicate at all times with God. Some may pray night and day (I Tim 3:10), and others just during the day but they are praying.

Are you wondering what position you should take in prayers? Hannah prayed with her mouth closed (I Sam 1:12-13) and it was answered (I Sam 1:26). Solomon prayed with his eyes opened during a convention (I Kings 8: 22-60; 2 Chr 6:1-42) and it was answered (2 Chr 7:1-3). Group prayers are accepted (Acts 12:12) and praying as a group simultaneously (Lk 1:10). Daniel prayed kneeling three times a day, and gave thanks to God, as he did aforetime (Dn 6: 10) and it was answered (Dn 6;20-28). Jesus did not have problems with people praying while standing (Mk 11:25). When Jesus was being baptized, he was praying, and the prayer was answered (Lk 3:21-22). That means; you can be working or driving and praying because God is everywhere. You can pray alone (Mk 1:35). Even in a group, seek private time to pray by yourself (Lk 9:18; 11:1; Mk 14:32). Paul prayed alone (Acts 11:5). You can pray in the Holy Ghost (Jude 1: 20). The only way to avoid temptation is to watch and pray (Mt 26:41). Jesus went into the mountain to pray (Mk 6:46). The only way to get things from God is by prayers (Mk 11:24). Some people could serve the Lord in prayers night and day (Lk 2:37). That is a calling just like some are called to preach and teach.

So why are you crying to human beings when you can pray to God who owns everything? People with problems should pray (Lk 5:33) and do all that a human being was supposed to do. What do you lack that you think God does not have? You make me shake my head left to right. But, if your hands are full with blood, God will not hear your prayers (Is. 1:15). Long prayers are not necessarily good prayers (Mk 12:40).

Until then, pray without ceasing.

Chapter Three

The Battles I fought and The Races I Ran

I have fought many battles: some I have lost and others I have won. I have run many races: some I have finished and others I dropped out. That is the way life is. In so far as I live on earth, there are and will be many battles for me to fight and many races for me to run. All I have to do is to select my battles and races I think to have the best chances.

As a young man I did not know which battles to fight and which races to run. Yet my father taught me one thing: those who reject some of your opinions openly and secretly and those who compete with you for real and as friends will leave a lasting impression in your life. As I make a flashback, their secret and public rebukes made me who I am today. Fearing they berate me, I strove to carry the mantle they all expected.

Lord, what would my life have been if I did not have the battles to fight and races to run? The battles we fight and win, and the races we run and finish make us rejoice. The battles we fight and lose should not make us bitter because everything works for the good of them that love God; rather, they should make us better. Those races we run but do not fish should not daunt us in life rather they should persuade us to improve better.

In this world we need each other to work as a team. The parents should work with the teachers and the students so the kids will receive a better education. The doctors should team up with insurance companies and patients to provide a better health care. The lawyers should work with the judges and those who need justice to provide a better justice system.

Therefore, let me ask you this: why do you feel bad when people criticize you? I am making a balanced sheet of my battles and races and all of a sudden I am developing a very high admiration for those with whom we fought some battles and competed in races. I know they made me better in tolerance, patience and perseverance because of the criticisms and the encouragements they gave me.

Until then, Lord I thank you for every human being you ever brought on my path.

Chapter Four

Friends in Deed And Need

A student came to me one day crying that one girl had slapped her. I asked for the name of her attacker, and she told me. So I said: "methought that is your friend?" She shook her head in a slow motion nodding; up and down in affirmation. Then I asked what happened? She replied: "she said I am saying things behind her back". Then today as I was reading through Patricia's blog, I found out that she had written about Bill Richardson: governor of New Mexico; a supposed friend of the Clintons who endorsed senator Obama. Thus the seed for this message is born.

A music seller told me a story one day. He pointed to the cemetery and said: "when you sit in front of this store, you learn lessons you may never forget. One of them was when a rich man died, and they were taking him to the cemetery. In his hearse was only a dog as his friend. He had no one because he had alienated himself from them. The dog sat with him looking very unconcerned and bewildered." Perhaps you all read in August 29, 2007 that Leona Helmsley left 12 millions for her dog, and her human chauffeur had $100,000. It is dysfunctional when the warmth of an animal replaces that of humans. It is a verbal picture that portrays the human being walking with his/her head down and his/her legs up. Some people have made friends with animals. Are human beings finished on earth?

We used to have our little dog (Babuel) that grew up with us. The day it died, we gave it a befitting burial. However, when it was alive, it never replaced the warmth of human beings.

When you find anything good the first people to tell should be your friends. I wonder then why some people call others their friends and are jealous of them. To sleep and seize your friend's wife (like what Samson's friend did) is not a sign of friendship (Jg 14:20).

Some people say they don't have friends. To make friends you must show yourself friendly (Prov 18:24). If you stick out for a good friend they will do same for you. A friend in need is a friend indeed. Do unto others what you want them do unto you. If you want loyal friends you should be loyal. If you want people to speak honest things to you then be honest to them. Make friends with people that can make you better because iron sharpenth iron (Prov 27:17)

True friends walk together (Gen 26:26). A good friend is a person through whom you can send something, and it reaches its destination (Gen 32:20). Good friends should be able to speak face to face (Ex 33:11). A good friend shares his or her spoils with his or her friends (I Sam 30:26). The friend of your friend is your friend (2 Sam 3:8). It is absurd to hate one's friend but love his enemies. True friends are the people that you should first call when you are faced with a calamity (Est 5:10; 6: 13).

The question is can anyone trust you as a true friend? Can they call you when they need your help or you will pretend you did not hear their call and then call after the incident has subsided? When friends are propping you about your calamity don't fret because they are acting only on the limited information they have (Job 32:3). When the time comes, they will pay for their rashness (Job 42: 7). True friends should be there whenever you need comfort (Job 2:11). A major characteristics of a true friend is faithfulness (Prov 27:6)

Therefore, any friend who flatters his or her friend, even the eyes of his children shall fail (Job 17:5). A true friend should love you at all times; no matter what you are going through (Prov 17:17). Take note of those lovers, friends and kinsmen who stand aloof of your sore. Those are bloodsuckers and parasites. It is true the poor is hated even by his neighbors, but the rich has many friends (Prov 14:20;

19:4, 7, 9). Why does the rich have many friends? Like bees they come to suck the nectar he or she has.

A man marries a beautiful woman, she makes an accident, and the next day he is divorcing her. Or perhaps they get married, and infertility sets in. The next day he wants another woman. This time he wants a woman that can give him children. Many men have had friends who were not working. When they found a job, they abandoned their friends and told them how they have moved up one class. What of the woman that was brought into a country by a man and when she is fine, she dumps the man calling him baboon.

People should learn how to keep their friends. If you want to keep your friends: avoid whispers (Prov 16:28) and avoid people who repeatedly offend you (Prov 17:9). When your friends start to fall under the sword, then look at your life. Is there anything you should have done to rescue the situation? Friendship fails because people cut away from God. God is the Only One that gives loyalty. When people do not live right, they cut off from the source of loyalty and no wonder promises and vows mean little or nothing to them. When a lover and a friend are put far away from you, know that you are going through the consequences of your sins (Ps 88:18).

Today let me confirm that human friends do fail no matter how loyal they may be. Yet there is a friend in Jesus who will bear your grieves and share your sorrows. In the middle of the night when everyone else is asleep, He will be by your side. Call Him in times of trouble and He will answer you. When it seems the whole world has misunderstood you, know that Jesus knows you and knows your name. Are you looking for a true and ever present friend? Get more in touch with Him. If you know the friendship of Jesus, he will give you the ability to make good and reliable friendship.

Until then, may you find trustful and worthy friends.

Chapter Five

Do You Think You Need Perfusion?

In 1993, a neighbor's child was seriously sick. They informed us after we returned from our preaching expedition from a village. Immediately we ran to the hospital to challenge the illness in prayers. When we arrived, the child was doing better. So I asked the doctor what was wrong, and he told us that the child merely needed some perfusion. I thanked the doctor, prayed for the child and wished him rapid recovery. Do you think your life needs a little bit of perfusion? Do you think the American economy needs some perfusion? Look around you; are you satisfied with what you see and feel, or do you think we need a little perfusion?

Recently an English teacher committed suicide. A month and May 29, 1999, Mark Barton lost his stocks and went on a rampage killing 9 and injuring 13. Last year an article published that teachers in the US are the highest victims of hypertension. Don't you think all these people needed a little perfusion?

People look at you and tell you how you look gorgeous but deep in you, you know you are sick. There is that sickness that seems to be ruffling your bones. The US Census Bureau statistics unveiled that the American Healthcare system currently leaves more than 45 million uninsured and does not cover people when they truly need it for they will have to seek permission from their insurance companies to see if they will cover that disease or this disease. He is the only doctor I know heals all diseases (Mt 9:35) and does not need insurance. Yes, that is your perfusion: real trust in Jesus!

Someone is crying there alone in secret because his or her relationships have never materialized to anything. The people you love and have invested into their lives ended up disappointing you. Relationships these days have been hijacked by technology and can easily be disposable just as technology is. Many have tried the friends with benefit, booty calls, and many others to no avail; they have always ended in a dead-end. Say: "I need a little perfusion: real trust in Jesus"!

Families are breaking apart than before, and friendships are dissolving faster than one ever thought. Feasts are organized, but trouble tears them up. It is high time for us to consider our ways and make our paths straight. In times of trouble, some will count on money, but now the money is failing. You would have counted on family, but they have abandoned you. Your friends are friends in deed are not friends in need. I tell you one thing: you need a little perfusion: trust Jesus from whence comes our hope.

Since I was young and now I am getting old I have never seen a righteous man or woman forsaken neither his nor her seed begging bread. I know how you struggle hard to give them a future but would you think the people whose savings have vanished in most of these financial crises did not have their children at heart? They did but despite their good intentions, man and things will always fail. Forget about the blame game; the bottom line is that the economy is soon entering into a serious comatose and needs some perfusion.

According to foreclosures.com 3 out of 1000 homeowners lost their homes in 2008. Molly PriesMeyer of the Minesota Independent revealed that, 283 lenders have collapsed since 2006. In September 5, 2008 the Labor Department announced that "Businesses shed 84,000 jobs in August as the unemployment rate soared to a five-year peak of 6.1%". These days even hardworking people seem to lack jobs because of the state of the economy. Those that have are uncertain when theirs will end. The creditors are pounding your phones; making you are scared to answer even calls from friends. You seem to be counting the least dollars in your account and wonder where next the other will show up. Go back again and take solace in the story of the widow (1 Kings 4: 1-7). You only need a little perfusion: real trust in Jesus!

If one is never down then they are supernatural but to be downcast should not make you cast down. If situations knock you down, refuse to be knocked out. Like a boxer, struggle and beat the bell. Only cowards commit suicide. It is honorable to die while fighting than die trying to flee. Do you remember that verse: "the just shall live by faith" (Hab 2:4)? Publicize in public his name and in secret keep his name sacred. That is the trust we need in Jesus. When everything else is failing around you, and the center can no longer hold, increase your vespers and lauds, and beef up your intercessions and supplications. It is not a time to give up; for only cowards give up. If you were to be renamed, would your last name be Coward? If no, why do you want to give up then? Many are the afflictions of the righteous, but the Lord always; I mean always delivers him or her from them all. Take that perfusion, and it shall be well with you.

Until then I wish you rapid recovery.

Chapter Six

Why Hide Your Sins?

Arabian Nights? Entertainment! Boys and girls I have a very nice Bible story from Gen 38:1-38 to tell you. There was a man in Israel called Judah. He married Shuah and had three sons: Er, Onan and Shelah. Judah married a wife (Tamar) for his son (Er). Due to his wickedness, the Lord slew him. His younger brother (Onan) inherited his wife. Because he did not want to have children in his brother's name, he decided to spill his seed on the ground. So the thing displeased the Lord, and He slew him too. Rather than Judah giving his daughter in law to his third son when he was marriageable, he decided to leave her lonely. She disguised as a harlot and seduced him. She then took some security deposit until he brings the promised kid.

When he reached home, he sent one of his friends an Adullamite to take the kid to the "harlot". Before he arrived there, she had left. He searched but could not see her. Three months later, he was told that his daughter in law Tamar had done prostitution and is even pregnant. Judah ordered that she should be brought to town and burnt alive. In her defense, she presented all the security deposit that Judah had given her and told the people that the owner was the author of her pregnancy. Thus, prostitution was not done alone. Judah confessed and repented of his evil. He acknowledged that she was more righteous than him who has refused to give her to his youngest son. She later had twins: Pharez and Zarah.

This is s classic story of hypocrisy where politicians pass laws and preachers preach against sin in public, but they do just the opposite. Then later they try to conceal their evil.

God has taught us that it is not just enough to acknowledged our sins when in danger and when danger starts to subside we run back to the same thing like Pharaoh used to do (Ex 9:27, 34) you must desire to change. In the OT, the reward for sin was so draconian that people feared and kept their sin secret. In the New Testament, the dispensation of grace gives humanity a great opportunity to come out open when we sin so that we may obtain mercy.

Many people have sinned; some revealed their sins but others were only exposed. You and I know that there are many people who hide their sins. When you confess and forsake your sins, God will always hear your prayers (I Kings 8:35-36, 46-47). So why do people hide their sins? After all, secrecy before humanity is an open book before God.

We hide our sins to shield our social status from our own hypocrisy (Gen 38: 2-26). You can remember preachers and politicians who voted for a law and were after charged and convicted of the same law. Spite and rancor make presidents of developing countries fear to leave power. With God, he rolls your sins into the bottom of the sea (Mic 7:19-20).

Despite encouragements from God that if people confess and forsake their sins they will have mercy (2 Chronicles 7:14), people still hide their sins.

It all began when Adam and Eve sinned. They ran and covered themselves with fig leaves (Gen 3:7; 10). Fig leaves are symbolic of an unauthentic covering. That is why God will later kill a lamb to use the skin and cover their nakedness (Gen 3:21) because for them to be properly covered, there must be a shedding of Blood. There is no remission of sins without the shedding of Blood (Heb 9:22). Yet, although there is possibility to repent of our sins and say we are sorry, people still prefer to cover them.

The reason why people cover their sins is the fear of disappointing those who look up to you (Gen 3: 7- 11). Adam and Eve were ashamed to fail God who loved them by created them, and trusted them by making them the caretakers of the garden.

Yet, again in the OT, God advised the people that if they sinned and it was found out, they should bring a sacrifice (Lev 4:14), or if they found out themselves that they have sinned then they should offer a sacrifice (Lev 4:23). No matter how we try to hide our sins, they will find us out (Num 323:23). The evil that men do, live with and after them.

The time has passed when parents died for the sins of their children or vice versa (2 Chr 25:4). Human beings must realize that they were sharpened in iniquity, and their mothers conceived them in sin (Ps 51:5). David once complained that: The LORD looked down from heaven upon the children of men, to see if there were any that did understand, and seek God. They are all gone astray, they are all together become filthy: there is none that doeth good, no, not one (Ps 14:2-3). If we confess and forsake our sins, we will have mercy (Prov 28:13). It is not only our sins but akso the sins of our people that we need to confess (Dan 9:20). If we confess our sins, he is faithful and just to forgive us our sins, and to cleanse us from all unrighteousness. If we say that we have not sinned, we make him a liar, and his word is not in us (I Jn 1:9-10).

So then should we continue to sin because there is grace? God forbid! (Rom 6:1)! There are some sins that we need to rebuke in public and not cajole and pamper. Excuses why anyone sinned should not be encouraged (I Tim 5:20). Rather, they should be exhorted to confess and forsake their sins lest they be hardened in sin (Heb 3:13). No matter your sin, there is enough grace to abound (Rom 5:20). God will always have compassion. The prodigal son's anecdote testifies to this (Lk 15:18, 21).

Until then, may our lives be opened books through which cronies and strangers may read the familiar and strange matters of life.

Chapter Seven

Does Your New Year Match Your New Year Wishes?

The year will be coming to an end, and everyone remembers 2008. It was a year with many dark series that reached the paroxysm with collapsed of Wall Street and the financial power houses. The world economies took a tumble and jobs visited the Pacific Ocean for good. You were not at Wall Street, but you know or heard of someone close who lost a job. You are not homebound but know someone who is. The bills have given you sleepless nights and made you run away from supposed creditors. Love deserted you by the finger, and it still stays an enigma why you cannot find lasting love. Deep in you, you wonder if you are cursed and think perhaps there is something you were not doing right. See, you will soon tear another calendar and for a lady there is Men o Pause or call it menopause while the men soon realize their equipments are not operating as they should and the doctors call it ED. The future is very bleak; I mean really gloomy.

Wars here and terrorists attacks there; dictators here and revolutions there; somewhere here, someone is crying for losing all they had, and somewhere there, someone is weeping for losing power. Indeed, cries nowadays surpass laughs, and the future may even augur a gloomier omen. Perhaps it is high time to seek refuge somewhere. Both young and old are now deep down into the fetters of drug addiction that it is now a hobby and not a deviation. Crime is now a tool in the survival kit for all ages.

While some people have a wish list of material things, others silently cry for help for their souls. The

Hollywood stars have shown us that material things do not make us happy. As you know; despite all their wealth, one thing: true love, has eluded most. That is top of their New Year wish List.

Young girls and boys are running into prostitution and scammers are perfecting their skills. Never in the history of this country and the world has life been so precarious especially for those who have lost their retirement benefits and for an individualistic society like ours. Then the cost of healthcare does not seem to abate anytime soon neither does sickness thinks of giving us a break. Good health seems to be in abeyance and obesity stairs a once skinny kid on the bed. Boy; the future really looks bleak!

Perhaps you will soon enter the New-Year and no one knows what will happen. Many went to sleep but never woke up, and many more will follow the same pattern before January 2013. You are the privileged one; indeed privileged reading me now. What have you done to be living until today? What is really special about you?

You have not had everything you wanted but at least you are happy having one more year. The future is very bleak as you can tell with all the gloom overshadowing world economies, but look unto Jesus the author and finisher of our faith. If you are knocked down don't remain on the floor to be knocked out, beat the bell as you look into the future with hope and anticipation. This God we serve walks with a pace unfamiliar to men, but it is sure and steady leading you unto a good port. Fret not when you see your friends and others you know acquiring wealth for that does not mean they are happy. They may be laughing without but weeping within; desiring they were instead like you. See, you have a lot of potentials, and the sky indeed should be your limit if you do not derail. Only cowards usually give up in life and ligate themselves to destinies which are not theirs for fear the future casts them down.

Dear, if you seek God first; all other things will be added unto you and by the time another year comes up, your joy will be full. Pray that you will not experience premature death and that you will not lose anyone to drug addiction. Pray that your joy will always be full despite the worries around. Pray that God will give you a health of steel. Pray that rather than see a gloomy future, you see one of hope and anticipation. All of this, ask in the Name of Jesus the reason for this Christmas celebration.

Until then, may you live long and happy!

Chapter Eight

LORD, I WANT TO BE A NAZARITE (Numbers 6:1-9):

When we look at people today who say they are Christians, we wonder if they really mean what they are saying. Do they really believe in God or are they really committed. Are they committed to their church or even God at all? Surely, if we are committed then we will depend on God for power, then we will die to self and finally we would avoid impurities. The purpose of this lesson is to whet our appetite to commitment in the Lord. If each of us is dedicated in the Lord as a nazarite we will influence our society in a twinkle of an eye and fill our churches with disciples. Let us go through Numbers 6:1-9 and see what God has in store for us.

The term nazarite comes from the Hebrew word *nazar* which means to dedicate. The Nazarites were known with their uncut hair, abstinence from wine and avoidance of dead bodies which were external signs of his vow. It should not be forgotten that Nazarites and priests were the only group of people with the injunction not to drink wine. He was regarded as the source of salvation to their aggressive neighbors. The vow changed in status from eternal to a given period of time which was marked by some ceremonial offerings as we see in Numbers 6 and Acts 21:24.

The Nazarite vow was taken by personal choice, by parents Judges 13:4-14; I Sam.1:11, or divine charism Amos 2: 11

:

Unction not Suction (Verses 3-4)

Exposition:
Wine was a regular present at the Jewish table during dinner. It was used for a drink offering (Ex. 29:40), make the heart merry (Est. 1; 10; Ps. 104:15); those who are sad (Prov. 31:6) and during feasts (Eccl. 10:19, Jn. 2). Yet, God gives as a condition that he should not drink wine, nor anything that was wine related. So by deduction wine was some sort of external influence to procure internal happiness. They could have something extra for their troubling souls through wine. Some went to the extent of getting drunk.

Application:
Nowadays, many people are so consumed by their daily encounters that they turn elsewhere for happiness. The Bible says that only the heathens worry (Mt. 6: 32). Kids are frustrated with their parents and they run away from home. Husbands are disappointed with the angelic bride they wedded yesterday and vice versa. Each of them looks towards drugs or alcohol or cigarettes for that inner peace. Listen to me; the Bible says that: "Peace I leave with you, my peace I give unto you: not as the world giveth, give I unto you. Let not your heart be troubled, neither let it be afraid" (Jn 14:27). How many people say when they are angry and they smoke a stick of cigarette they come back to normal? Now listen: "These things I have spoken unto you, that in me ye might have peace. In the world ye shall have tribulation: but be of good cheer; I have overcome the world" (Jn. 16:33). A president or governor sees their only son parading the neighborhood as an addict. They cannot take it. It should be the child of the poor alien that should walk down that stretch. He cannot figure out so he turns to the bottles to calm his worries, youngsters smoke weed to gain the courage to talk to people. Ministers drink to levels of intoxication to be able to face the crowd. They lack the anointing and so visit mystiques, fortune tellers or sorcerers

for special powers to move the crown and heal the sick. Senators, ministers, directors, CEOs are married to syringes to keep with the headaches of their workplaces. Hollywood stars and talk show hosts are embroiled with tranquilizers and sex to find the deluded happiness. The military swims in drug and alcoholism to diffuse and minimize the presence of death. In seeking those external influence to appease their carnal cravings they are in fact inviting death "For to be carnally minded *is* death; but to be spiritually minded *is* life and peace" (Rom. 8:6). Jesus told the disciples to wait in Jerusalem till the received the Holy Spirit so that he would empower them for the ministry. By our strength alone we can do nothing.

Illustration:

A missionary was sent to China. He moved there with his wife and kids. Then by a stroke of fate his first son was dead. In addition to his frustrations he could not win a soul. So he slumped into alcohol. Then after some time became an alcoholic. He divorced the wife and went back to the US to live his drunken life.

Mr. Brown was a graduate from a renowned university in the US with a doctorate in mathematics. He got involved with drugs to cope with the new standard of life Hollywood propagates for people of his status. Gradually he became an addict, lost his job, the sky soon became his sole covering, resorted to using only his two legs for errands and his body was a sample of a derelict.

On the contrary Samson, Samuel, John the Baptist and Paul when faced with the same situation relied on the Spirit to overturn impossible situations. Samson defeated his enemies each time the Spirit came on him. Samuel was an anointed priest. John the Baptist set fear in the hearts of evildoers and Paul was a threat to both Rome and the Sanhedrin. So let us avert external excitation to fulfill our inner satisfaction on the contrary let us be filled with the

Holy Spirit through whom we obtain all the comfort we need to face the challenges of life.

Inner Man versus the Show Business Man (Verse 5)

Exposition:
Hair was very important in Israelis dressing. However at a given time to set a difference with the pagans the Jews cut their hair real low down but not to conform to the heathen standards. To show a difference for those who wanted to enter into the Nazarite vow they had to leave their hair untouched. That is; never cut a hair out of it nor trim their beards. Also if they were mourning they would not trim their beards. So Samson not cutting his hair rang a bell to those who saw him. That meant that he was to live from the inner strength. That showed he was to die to self so that the strength that has not been corrupt could be displayed through him.

Application:
Here we see the concept of dying to self to e great in works of the Spirit. Therefore, what is dying to self? Dying to self is when a reckless driver cuts in front of you on the high way and you do not curse them. When people talk about you and you do not get angry. When people pay your good with evil and it does not irritate you. When your daughter dates another color and you do not want to hang. When your paycheck skips a day and you do no promise to cut off the head of the manager. When you are wrongfully fired and you do not think of settling your scores with an AK 47 and grenades. Dying to self is being happy what the food mama put on the table, happy with the clothes on your back and graceful to the shoes on your feet (though they are not in fashion). Dying to self is when you do not jealous the sister who sings more than you crow. Dying to self is when you do not nurse any evil feelings about the alien because you think they have come to take your jobs. Dying to self is when the

husband can drop that remote control for some time for the woman to hold it too. When parents can accept rebukes from their kids. When kids accept their mistakes and seek advice from their parents. Have you died to self? Would a corpse feel bad what people say about them? Would a dead person feel bad if the husband was giving something to the needy relative? Would the corpse complain about the lotion the mortician is uses on them? About the type of casket the family bought for them? If not why do you complain about the house you live, the brand of car you drive, the color your daughter should marry? Where is the dying to self when the minister has three cars and a plane for himself? Here is the dying to self when we buy food and stock in the refrigerator when we cannot even use? Where is dying to self when we make fun of the poor neighbor's kids? Yes where is dying to self when we fight among ourselves. Can dead people fight? Where is dying to self when we cannot live or share a room with another person? Where is dying to self when there is a particular car you must drive else the divorce court will host us? The Bible says let us: "But now we are delivered from the law, that being dead wherein we were held; that we should serve in newness of spirit, and not in the oldness of the letter" (Romans 7:6). Paul again repeats that: "So then they that are in the flesh cannot please" (Rom. 8:8). Jesus said: "And whosoever doth not bear his cross, and come after me, cannot be my disciple" (Lk. 14:27). So likewise, whosoever he be of you that forsaketh not all that he hath, he cannot be my disciple (Lk 14:33).

Illustration:

Ginger Boyd left the US and went to Cameroon with other Christians as a missionary. First, she did not live in the Little US in Cameroon (the fenced neighborhood most of the other missionaries from the US live in). She rented and shared a room with another missionary called Carrie Taylor. Both ladies lived in that place until they left Cameroon. Ginger even went further north to meet a people that seem less developed to those in Yaoundé. Her chances of meeting the man of her life are reduced to nothing with her life at the mercy of these villagers, yet because she knew and knows God is with her, it meant nothing living with those who could easily harm her because when a man's ways please the Lord, He makes even his enemies to be at peace with him. (Prov. 16:7)

Dead to sin alive in Christ (Verses 6-9).

Exposition:

In Israel the people were not supposed to touch even dead animals and if a dead animal touched a human or anything that they touch, it too shall be untouchable (Lev.11:31, 32).They were not to mourn the dead by cutting themselves. As for the priest God went again further by saying they were not supposed to touch even the corpse of the dad, mum not any other dead body. And his relatives were not to touch the dead also.

The apostle Paul explains it to the Corinthians when he says "O death, where *is* thy sting? O grave, where *is* thy victory? The sting of death *is* sin; and the strength of sin *is* the law." (I Cor. 15:55-56). In that sense each person would strive to avoid sin which is the cause of death.

Application: You should write an application.

Illustration: Write an illustration.

Chapter Nine

When God's People Overcome a Bad Year

Are there people fighting you? Are there situations in your life that have made you once or many times ponder on suicide? Are you fighting with a terminal disease? Perhaps you are struggling hard to divorce solitude. Are there people at work who hate you, or neighbors who threaten you with death? Are there relatives that think you should have been dead, or friends who are jealous of your success and plot against you? Today I bring you a message of hope and challenge.

You see; "... from the days of John the Baptist until now the kingdom of heaven suffers violence, and the violent take it by force" (Mt 11:12). Today, I want you to start the New Year with the determination not to let anyone or anything push you around. The recession is bringing a lot of bad news and many will be pushed over. Will you be standing or knocked out? I will narrate some Bible examples of people who did not allow bad situations and people to take life away from them, so you should not too!

Israel was in bondage for 400 years when Moses was sent to liberate them. When Pharaoh wanted to annihilate them, God turned the seabed into a highway and the water as parapets to the Israelites; although, that same water became a watery grave for the Egyptians. In 2013, God will convert your dangers into savers. Amen!

Is the country not going the way God wants? You know you will not change it by being fearful and afraid. Rise up mighty soldier of valor and do what God is telling you now.

Let 2013 be a year when you rent young lions that roar at you, and you eat from the same situations that first threatened you; consequently, turning your stumbling blocks into staircases.

No matter how wicked Ahab was, it was Elijah who had the last laugh. Children of God, will you shout alleluia? While Ahab prepared for battle by eating and drinking (in the flesh) Elijah prepared up Mount Carmel; like a woman giving birth (in the spirit) (I Kings 18:18). Indeed giving birth to a new beginning. Children of God, the wickedness in 2013 will only be overcome by the spirit.

Your 2012 tormentor could have been like Goliath with all the armor but do not forget that little David defeated him. Goliath had almost all the physical armor mentioned in Ephesians 6: 10-18, but he lacked prayers and supplications. You will win because the battle is not by might nor by power but by the Spirit of the Lord.

Listen: you suffered from racism and its collusions. Don't worry; remember that Haman fell into the gallows he built for Mordecai. God will always deliver you from the snare of the fowler and noisome pestilence.

There are some of you whose greatest trials and temptations came from your own family, and that you seem like the enemy in the house. Oh well, do you remember Jehpthah who was driven away by his half brothers? When the Philistines, and then later the Ammonites attacked them, the Gileadites sought him as their general (). So I tell you; dither not, for there will be time when you will command their respect. The stone that the builders reject always ends up becoming the cornerstone.

Perhaps you are a student and mates are making fun of you. God will mock those who mock you; for they end up as shredded meat in the hands of bears (). They have declared a war against God and not you because whoever touches you touches the apple of God's eye ().

Nowadays everyone seems to be a prophet of the Lord, and they prophesy what people want to hear. Those that do not preach what the society wants to hear are labeled false prophets, but false prophets acclaimed greats. That did not start today. Think of Zedekiah and Micaiah. Micaiah remained true to God only saying what God asked him to say and not what the people wanted to hear. When the time of reckoning came, he was justified ().

Perhaps some government authority is frightening you, and you are ready to leave town. King Jeroboam may narrate his ordeal. The same hand they point at you shall paralyze, and they will ask you to entreat the Lord your God for their recovery.

At times people just don't like you, so they accuse you for nothing especially in modern times that God is a burden to the society. When you make God your delight, the fire of false accusation shall not consume you. Rather, your accusers will be cut in pieces, and their houses shall be made a dunghill as was the case with Shadrach, Meshach, and Abednego who were falsely accused before Nebuchadnezzar.

Other people just envy you because you are smart and do things better than them. Here is your consolation: even when you are cast into the den of lions like Daniel, the angel of the Lord shall shut the lions' mouths, that they don't hurt you: forasmuch as before Him innocence is found in you before the law. Your accusers will take the punishment they had conspired for you.

The Pharisees tried with Jesus, but although they killed the body, he resurrected after three days and went to heaven where he will judge the living and the dead. The power in you cannot be bought with money. That is why you should consider yourself great. Those who try to prevent you from spreading the word end up as blind Barjesus.

Is the Bible still true? Has it changed? Don't you read that the same God yesterday is the same today and the same forevermore ()? Every little situation has beaten you up, and every little difficulty has given you depression. Are you a Christian? Is God still carrying your burdens, or are you casting them on yourself? You were beaten in 2012 because you did not put your full armor of God. I say put on the whole armor of God. Fear ye not, standstill, and see the salvation of the LORD, which he will show to you today: for the enemies whom ye have seen in 2012 ye shall see them again no more forever. The LORD shall fight for you, and ye shall hold your peace.

Until then, make the Lord your delight and 2012 will be under your control.

Chapter Ten

Worthwhile Ending the Old Year and starting the New Year in Church?

Every year there are a couple of traditions that are scrupulously followed. So 2011 was not different. On New Year's Eve, people spend the rest of the seconds or even hours in a church because they want to end the Old Year and start the New Year with God. Great job; no problem at all! Then there are those with New Year resolutions. But before then there are many who have sent out peace and New Year wishes. This morning I will consider these three traditions so that you see the futility or utility in all that we do. There is a reason why despite us starting the year in church that year did not bring us any good. Do you want me to tell you why?

What is the need of wishing Happy New Year to someone you do not want to see or smell? There are some people you wished "Happy 2011" but until the year elapsed, you neither spoke with them nor try to enquire how the year was going for them. Then this year you are doing the same tradition sending cards, emails and text messages. Wilt thou know, O vain people that faith without works is dead? Why do people wish someone they have been quarrelling with peace without extending a hand of peace in the New Year? Wouldn't the peace start from them?

One common tradition that the majority does is going into the church to start the year. First let me state that with the death of Jesus, the temple of God shifted from a building to the human body. Thus, the best way is to dedicate or rededicate your body for those who have not done that. The church is supposed to be clean, but you and I know that nowadays the church is more a den of thieves; looking to pilfer and swindle from you rather than seek to safe your soul from damnation. Your house could be holier than the church. It would even be nice to stay at home with your family and pray to God because you know how you live, but you do not know how the next person lives. You repent of your sins, but the next person may not be willing, and their presence is merely hindering prayers because "if I regard iniquity in my heart, the Lord will not hear me" (Ps 66: 18).

Therefore, call your enemies and apologize to them. Tell them if you wronged them that they should forgive you. Write down a list of your peccadilloes and shortcomings of 2011, then confess and determine to forsake them, so you could obtain mercy. If you want all other things to be added unto you this 2012, then you must seek ye first the kingdom of God and its righteousness.

You and I know it is no righteousness to seize someone's husband or wife. There is no righteousness in not talking with your parents for years because you are mad. Where is the righteousness in stealing from your neighbor and sending him on retirement with nothing? Would you tell me the righteousness in doing drugs? So do you see why the previous years, though we started them in church; nevertheless, they brought us no peace and happiness?

We have been trekking too far to search, seek or knock on doors for things that are beside us. Every year you made 20 New Year resolutions but each year finishes with you on number 4. O fear the LORD, ye his saints: for there is no want to them that fear him (Ps 34:9). I have been young, and now am old; yet have I not seen the righteous forsaken, nor his seed begging bread (Ps 37:25). And Jesus answered and said, Verily I say unto you, There is no man that hath left house, or brethren, or sisters, or father, or mother, or wife, or children, or lands, for my sake, and the gospel's, But he shall receive an hundredfold now in this time, houses, and brethren, and sisters, and mothers, and children, and lands, with persecutions; and in the world to come eternal life (Mk 10:29-30).

Until then, seek God; the Giver of 2009 and your year will be wonderful.

Chapter Eleven

Lord, My Womb Is Empty

This lesson is for the many women I have known who although married, have sought for a child to no avail. Some have had the raillery of society, and others of even their husbands who were supposed to protect and nurture them with love. Many have spent days and nights increasing their lauds and vespers to God, but they seem to have their prayers bounce back to them. Night and day they cry: "Lord my womb is empty".

Many at times I have been baffled why God gives children to women who do not want them but does not give to those who want them. At times I worry why some are having octuplets while others are unsuccessfully looking for merely one. I quiz myself how we will multiply and replenish the earth if women do not get pregnant. In this lesson, I will talk about women who were barren briefly and those who were barren for life.

Sarah; Abraham's wife was barren (Gen 11:30). It worried Abram the husband too that she was getting old without a child. He even slept with their amah to get pregnant, but God insisted he will have his own son. Sometimes we consider our situations hopeless especially when the woman has passed her period that we laugh at promises like Sarah did (Gen 18:11-15). God does not fail in his promises that at the appointed time Sarah had a baby at 90 (Gen 21:2). The Bible says it was by faith (Heb 11:11).

The second woman that was barren briefly was Rebekah: Isaac's wife (Gen 25:21). One thing strikes me though; in both of these cases their husbands stood with them. They (husbands) entreated the Lord even more while their wives did the crying. In most male chauvinistic societies, the woman bears all the blame and ignominy even when the man is the impotent one. These are difficult times for the woman, so they need more support than blame from their husbands.

The third case was that of Rachel: Jacob's wife (Gen 29:31). At times God closes those wombs so that he can commandeer love for others. Perhaps you did not like other people's kids, and God wants you to learn how to love the children of others. Sometimes if a woman cannot conceive, she envies those who can (Gen 30:1). Others nag their husbands for children day and night (Gen 30:1). Rachel later conceived (Gen 30:22-24). The children that women who have struggled to give birth born end up being stories of hope to humanity like Joseph.

Mrs. Manoah was barren (Judges 13:2-3), and the man entreated the Lord (Judges 13:8) because his wife's barrenness was not her problem alone; it was theirs both. Finally, the woman bore a son (Judges 13:24), and he grew up to be Samson the warrior! I told you children barren women give birth are usually the Hercules of the society.

The fifth case was Hannah (I Sam 1:5). Her adversary provoked her for being childless that she resorted to crying and starving herself. She took her bitterness to the priest; God's representative. Cast all your cares unto God for he cares for you (I Pet 5:8). At the appointed time, she had a child (I Sam 1:20). If you are not dead, please have hope.

The sixth case is the woman who had a very old husband who could not get her pregnant. Her kindness made the prophet intervene for her, and she later conceived (2 Kings 4: 8-17). Is your husband too old to fertilize your eggs? You should count on God! Impossible things to man are possible to God (Lk 18:27).

The seventh case was Elisabeth: the wife of Zechariah the priest who was barren (Lk 1:5-7). Note the emphasis that they were both righteous. That means barrenness is not synonymous to being sinful. So stop asking God what you have done that He does not want to give you children. Did you realize that women who are single have children? Thus, they are living in fornication. If children were based on righteousness, then they would not have because God is against fornication. But the ways of God are always strange! Although Zachariah was already an old man (Lk 1:18), the Lord gave them a child called John (Lk 1:57-63).

Nevertheless, there were other women in the Bible who though married died without having children. The first case was Michal: King Saul's daughter and King David's wife (2 Sam 6:20-23).

Therefore, there are a few things to remember. God is the one who gives children (Gen 4:1; Ps 127:3). People could take sperms and fuse them to fertilize the eggs but if God does not give his blessing they will come to naught. God can make a barren woman the mother of children again (Ps 113:9). God has promised your wife will be fruitful (Ps 128:3). Count on Him as I adapt Isaiah's promise!

> *Sing, O barren woman, you that has no child; break forth into singing, and cry aloud, thou that didst not travail with child: for more are the children of the desolate than the children of the married wife, says the LORD. For you are not desolate; be not ashamed or confounded. Forget the shame of your childlessness and don't remember the reproach of your barrenness. For your Maker is your husband. For the LORD has called you as a woman forsaken and grieved in spirit, and a wife of youth. For though God has hid his face in a brief moment from you with everlasting kindness will He have mercy on you. For the mountains shall depart, and the hills be removed; but His kindness shall not depart from you, neither shall the covenant of His peace be removed, says the LORD that has mercy on you. O thou afflicted, tossed with tempest, and not comforted, behold, He will lay your stones with fair colors, and lay you foundations with sapphires. In righteousness will you be*

*established: you will be far from oppression; for you
will not fear: and from terror; for it shall not come
near thee.*

Until then, weep no more for God sees your tears.

Chapter Twelve

Are You A Quitter or Go-Getter?

The Bible does not encourage Christians to be quitters. When you are faced with a disappointment, stick in there; for even your mockers will sympathize with you. Always turn your disappointments into opportunities. There was a young woman from Canada who was invited to sing the national anthem: *Star Spangled Banner* in a hockey game. She first forgot the lyrics to the song went back, recollected herself and as she came out, she stumbled on the staircase.

First she would have recognized that it was a one time opportunity for her not being American to be given the privilege to sing the American National Anthem in such a ceremony. She was neither the first one to have botched the anthem nor would she be the last. She was neither the first to fall nor would she be the last. She would have converted her disenchantments into serious blessings: a story of courage and persistence and next time who knows who might have invited her back for a bigger occasion.

If this young woman had finally taken out a paper from her pocket and sung the national anthem, she would have been the heroine of the ceremony. After all, there is no law that says you should not read the national anthem from a paper. After all, there is no law that says you should never fall? After all each and every one of us has fallen once in their life since they were born. Unfortunately, she allowed her drawback to reign over her.

On the contrary, there was a young woman who was running a marathon. Close to the finish line, she collapsed, but her determination to complete the race made her crawl to the finish line. Crawl to the finish line.

Why should you feel so disappointed that you want to give up your dream opportunity? When you succeed in a trial like that, you have taught others a lesson. Those trials that you overcome further the gospel, and the people in similar situations wax with confident and become bolder. You have just turned your disappointments into blessings.

My friends, learn to turn your disappointments into blessings. Stop carrying your problems on your head as if you are the only one with problems. Everyone has problems; they just don't carry them for you to see. Rather than carry them on your head, convert them into beautiful staircases.

Until then, only stop when you achieve your objective.

Chapter Thirteen

True Friendship

My friend asked me to write a story on true friendship, and I felt the best one would be about my best friend and I. We met in Full Gospel Tsinga Church, solidified our friendship while in CLUC and lived together. When my term in A2, Ngoa Ekelle hostel was up, I moved to Bonamoussadi to join him. Coming, I brought along another friend: Njoh Divine (who is now a pastor too). We (especially Divine) disagreed 90% of the time on doctrinal issues.

Other than our doctrinal differences, we never had problems. There was an entente that we would close our ears to rumors and slanders about us. Envious people who knew we were like bone and marrow did not like that. I was a leader in church, and both of them were not. I was a young leader; in fact the youngest of all the deacons and elders in those days. My detractors felt that they could use him as a bridge to the youths to dwindle my influence, but he refused to be cowered into being a turncoat. Each time they made their bundles of fabrications to him, our friendship bailed me out. Take note: constant communication was our secret. He and I went to the field to pray every morning, and other youths later joined us. The gendarmes picked us up twice while interceding there. Our greatest yearning was to trust each other always.

When he graduated from Ngoa Ekele, he went home to live as a farmer because he could not find work. It broke my heart! The day I was preaching, I rebuked the church for neglecting young people like him. An Elder: Claude Tchamda volunteered to join me financially too. Immediately I cashed in on my first job, I took the salary and went to bring him back. I did not tell him I was coming and had never been to his village before. I bought a bag of salt and carried some other necessary things that his mother will need when he left for the city. We then left for the city but not as Absalom Kumalo.

He buoyed my confidence as a trustworthy friend who defended me in truth though we had philosophical differences when I fantasized having him back in town. He was very faithful. His village does not have a motorable road, so one would have to walk for at least three hours. You caught a car from Yaoundé to Bot Makak. Then you walked to Mbonde: his village. I asked the driver, and he told me that it was just a stone throw. I did not know it was an understatement. After Bot Makak, I walked for one hour but did find the place. I asked the next villager who told me in French "C'est ne pas loin. Continue à marcher et des que tu traverse la petite rivière tu serais déjà la". By this time I was sweating from the weight of the salt and the other bags I had all over me. Villagers inquired whether I was going to pay the dowry because in their tradition one of the things you need to knock the door of a lady's parents is a bag of salt. I told them that I was going to see a friend who lives in Mbonde. Darkness threatened and the rain menaced. Don't we say if you carry salt don't walk under the rain? So I prayed and asked God to hold the rains until I reached. Then I increased my pace.

On arrival, he had gone to the farm. I sat there and waited until he returned. Then I told him that I had come to take him back to town. He resisted that the city was hopeless without a job especially because he does not like to be fed. He prefers here as a farmer. You know; he meant subsistence farming. His calling as a great pastor and excellent teacher had made me weep everyday. I felt bad losing him. I explained to him that he will go to school and become a pastor; that the church was going to support him.

I was already admitted in the Assemblies of God Bible School called West African Advanced School of

Theology (WAAST). I went to Jim Lemons-the director: a friend and a great missionary that I highly respected. He admitted Benjamin although the initial stages the school was meant only for English speakers which exempted Benjamin as a French speaker. Our Church: Full Gospel Nsimeyong II had accepted to pay his tuition. A new dawn has begun for my friend.

So let me ask you this? Are you a friend that someone can count on? Can your friend leave you with his wife or her husband and still not feel threatened? Do you have a friend you really trust that you know what he can say behind your back? If Benjamin said anything behind my back it was just praise and nothing but praise. If there was something he did not agree with me, he waited until we were going back home or at home then he said "mais pastor; toi même la tu as tort". He will never join your adversaries to crucify you. Nunca! We never loaned each other anything. We gave to each other according to his or her needs. We did not really differentiate clothes if not of the fact that my clothes were a bit bigger for him. I could wear his and still look a bit descent, but when he wore mine he was like a little squirrel in a lion's jacket.

When one of us was sick, the other went to look for medicine. I was really sick in 1994, he and Divine carried me to the hospital, but the doctors refused to treat me because they could not buy a ticket. So they brought me back where he prepared some herbs until I recovered. That was the last time I ever went to the hospital because I was sick. He kept joking with me that this one that you are sleeping in bed all day means that fever is really beating you. We were always there for each other. We respected our appointments (I Sam 20:35).

After some time, I left and came to the US. Benjamin continued and went to Togo where he graduated and pursued his graduate studies. He was strong in house work where I was really weak, but I knew how to make things happen. We visited Christians together, went to church together, ate together, and slept together (not as amorous lovers). The day

I was toppled from the University group while in Douala, I came, met him, but he did not say a word. That is how confident he was about me. He knew that I will definitely face it so why worry to tell me. When I went to the meeting, and they told me, I laughed as we walked back home. He told me I told them that that man would not even bother about it. Indeed, I did not. If you came to the house to ask for a favor, he knew what I will do and what I could not do. At times he spoke my heart in my absence. We went to help Christians with their farms together. Today he is married with children and a great district pastor with the Full Gospel Mission.

Don't worry that you don't agree in everything. Even if you were born in the same house, you will never agree 100%. Do you have a true friend: one that you know can put their life in jeopardy for you? If not then you can start by having Jesus: a trust and faithful friend. He will teach you what true friendship is. If you are a Christian but are allergic to faithfulness, then you should ask God for the fruit of the spirit. One of them is actually faithfulness.

Until then, be a faithful friend.

Chapter Fourteen

The God Who Was Never There?

Mothers Day was near, but I was not yet settled with what I would buy for my mother. So I began praying. I have told God I don't want to give someone anything they do not need. Most of my friends know that. So I began praying. I prayed and prayed but felt as if God was not answering my prayers. So one day I was sleeping when someone called me from home. I really don't like those calls but again I like them. Don't we say "if someone is not your own person, they will neither call nor write you." Although they wake me up from sleep, I still cherish those calls. If anyone told me never write me again or never call me again, or perhaps they say, "take my email off your list," That same hour, I delete and expunge it because I never deal with people who don't want me. So I consider those who communicate with me my own people.

Nonetheless, I could no more sleep, so I went on the net to search for gifts for this special Day. Lo and behold I saw a watch that was originally for about $856 now on sale for $78. So I decided to shop for the same product in eBay and ubid and other places to see if I will find it cheaper. I like cheaper prices but quality products. I went to Amazon and other places and compared the prices to make sure I was not someone's milky cow. All the places gave the upper hand to the price that I initially saw. So I bought it.

So it was Saturday and mom asked me if I know what day was tomorrow. I told her no. She said it is Mother's Day. Then she joked that if I got old, I will be terrible because I like to forget. So I asked her: "mom what do you want". She said there is only one thing that she wants. I said "don't tell me about sending money home to anyone. Tell me what you want and I will buy it." She said that she wanted only a watch.

Gainsayers will tell me it is coincidence. Those who know God say that it is a miracle of an answered prayer. The God we serve neither sleeps nor slumbers people. He hears each of us when we cry. When you are sad in your soul, crying in your spirit, or laughing because your problems are more than you could bear, Jehovah Jireh sees you and hears your cry. He will never fail those who trust him. God does not abandon those who have not abandoned him. Our God knows the intent of our hearts. For the great God is omnipresent and omniscient. I say Jehovah is a Man of war. He will fight your battles if you will cast your burdens unto Him. He is a man who truly cares. Yes, he does! Never and never give up; no matter how the tides may turn against you. Each time you kneel, the Merciful and Almighty God sees your chagrin.

Where are you, who says that God is no more there? Who says God has gone on a journey and has not returned? Did you hear my story? Do you see what he does daily in my life? Oh test and see how faithful and trustworthy our God is. He keeps his promises and fulfills even those he did not make to us. At times, he fulfills even the ones our hearts were still pondering about. Please test and see how the Lord is good.

Until then, Jesus never fails so trust in him with all your burdens.

Chapter Fifteen

My Mother Bought Me New Clothes

Part 1

Text: Colossians 3:5-4:6

1. Introduction:

There seems to be no difference today between the Christian and non Christian. Although they say they are now Christians, their behaviors have not changed. They still do the same things they were doing when they were non Christians. If anyone has believed, there must be a difference between his lifestyle before conversion and the one after conversion. There remains a question though: how should Christians live? Can we separate a Christian from a non Christian by their lifestyles? The purpose of this lesson is to whet our appetite to commitment in the Lord with a lifestyle that differentiates us from those who have not believed. How can we honor Christ's Lordship in our lives? The Christian will have to show that at home, in prayer, in relations to other Christians by imitating Christ, loving God and their neighbors: grooming the peace of God in their hearts, being always thankful and imbued in the word. This takes us to the title of today: "Put on New Clothes" taken from Colossians 3: 5-4:6. Let us read. Our first point today is Christ's Lordship in the Christian's life.

2. Christ's Lordship in the Christian life 3:5-3:17

A. Exposition:

The Christian command to apply Christ in our lives urges everyone to mortify their members. The word "mortify in verse 5" means to eliminate the over hangings or unwanted excesses of the flesh: those works of the flesh that will hinder us from serving God. By not serving God we walked (lived) in the wrath of God. We can avoid the wrath by shedding off the particulars of the Old man (worn out) to put on (as investing with clothing) the new man (regenerated). The old man is the sinful nature that is to be replaced with the regenerated person born again from the encounter of believing in Christ. That means; the old nature which is sin oriented is to be replaced with newness in life where Christ is the centre of attraction and meaning to our lives. The believer must then wear the elements of the new person just as clothes are worn. Within the human heart lies various conflicts, but the peace of Christ must rule (serve as the umpire or referee) so that we can enjoy life in abundance which comes with becoming a new creature in Christ.

B. Application:

We will divide this command of applying Christ's lordship in us into two: the particulars of the old man to dispose and the particulars of the new man to put on. It is important for us to know why we cannot keep the old man when we believe in Christ. Jesus said "No man putteth a piece of new cloth unto an old garment, for that which is put in to fill it up taketh from the garment, and the rent is made worse (Mt 9:17)". The Apostle Paul goes further to elucidate on what he meant by mortifying our members from the old man. The things that the old man carries are sexual uncleanness, covetousness, anger, wrath, blasphemy, malice and sins of speech. At the same time we are replacing the old man with the new man which is Christ centered: love, affection for one another, kindness, , humility, meekness, patience, bearing one another, forgiveness, and above all else, putting on signs of love.

C. Illustration:

A lady wanted to compensate her kids for guarding the house while she was on a trip. She bought them all new clothes. She called each of them to the bedroom to try them. But they must first pass her test before they took the clothes. Each of them left the room without the clothes. And when they asked her why she did not want to give them the clothes she told them that they did not appreciate her gift. If they did, they would have removed their old clothes first before putting the new ones. They had to take off first their old clothes before adorning themselves with the new ones. The new man will be called Christian living which is our second point.

Until then, put on true Christianity for the world to see.

Chapter Sixteen

THE UNCERTAINTY OF LIFE'S JOURNEY; JOSHUA 3: 1-3.

Crossing the journey of life is like crossing a major River on foot in its overflowing days. Life seems bleaker than it was yesteryears ago. We hate to look back at 2011 because we seem to see but not touch the American Dream. Hopes are slimmer and dreams are lost. Because we have suffered for too long, we drink fairytales on fairylands with insatiable gullibility. Depression is now a homemade product. Such was the case of the Israelites too. The children of Israel were promised Canaan on the other side of River Jordan. They did not know the way; never passed that road or been there before. Thus, they must rely on a guide. If they had to follow God, then they must be holy because He is holy (I Pet 1:15). They would do that through his priests. God will manifest himself in a pillar of cloud by day to keep them cool and a pillar of fire by night to keep them warm. By so doing the people knew that God was alive. Today I want to flashback at how the children of Israel crossed River Jordan and to lend you some principles that will help you make the journey of life joyfully because life is always a journey similar to that of the Israelites.

Similarity 1: looking for direction. Every human being is looking for direction some point in life; each looking for the square peg to fit in the square hole. They had to follow the priests and the Levites. Who are you following to lead you into the journey of life? I guess your counselor. Did you know that even the best counselor sometimes makes mistakes. Ahithophel the best did fail and committed suicide

(2 Sam 17:7; 23). Jesus says: "I am the way, the truth, and the life: no man cometh unto the Father, but by me" (Jn 14:6). Some people are used to not asking for directions, and they end up turning round and round the same road. Time wasted can never be regained. So, why not follow the Guide: Jesus that never loses direction.

The second similarity: a new road we have not passed there before. What human has lived the journey of life? None! So why do you court the psychic? Sylvia Brown made the news on The Montel Show when she told a woman that her boyfriend drowned. Much to Sylvia's shock, the woman revealed her boyfriend was a firefighter and died in the 9/11 terror attacks. Think of Tracy Higgs, John Edwards, British clairvoyant: Lisa Williams and the rest. If they knew how to win those Mega millions, they will not take the little dime you have to survive. None of them and no human with supernatural powers can predict to you all about your life because God alone is Omniscient.

Third similarity: the condition to sanctify ourselves. How do you live? Would you accept for your life to be placed on a giant screen for all to watch? The Nigerian 419 scams just showed America and the world how gullible and hypocritical we live with a doctor trying to wash money from black paper. Sorry Mugu! The people complained to Jeremiah about hardship, and he tells them that: "Your iniquities have turned away these things, and your sins have withholden good things from you (Jer 5:25)." The crocodile cannot go to the jaguar for food.

The fourth similarity: follow the priest and Levite. I know nowadays it would seem like the modern days priests and ministers need to follow the people rather than the people following them. Even so, would you pull off all your teeth because you have a bad tooth? There are many good prelates that we should follow than those going astray.

Fifth similarity: God is alive! God is among you. Does it look like God is with our world or it looks like he has abandoned us. If you trust God and follow His guidance, then impossible things to you will become possible. If God does not calm the storm, He will calm you in the storm.

The journey of life is a path we are all condemned to saunter. Yet what matters is how you go through. My hope is that we make the journey with joy and victory, and we would like to look back rather than regret why we were ever born.

Until then, count on God who knows your future.

Chapter Seventeen

A Shout Out To Jesus Christ: My Best And Most Trustworthy Friend!

Prophets prophesied that he will be very controversial, so old men waited to set their eyes on him before they died. He did not preach to please people; rather he told them "he that is not with me is against me." What manner of Man is this?

He was not a Bigman because he was born in a manger, yet emperors envied him. Although an adolescent, he debated and lectured law professors. He could ride any horse, but he trekked with those who served him. If he was in a hurry, he walked upon the sea. He could have lived in any mansion, but he did not have a home of his own just so He could feel the plight of the homeless and the destitute. What manner of Man is this?

He began alone, but He had thousands and still has millions of followers. Even though the only mediator between God and the world, he still prayed himself too to serve as a practical teacher. Through his prayer, 2 fish and five loaves of bread fed more than 15 thousand people. He was a carpenter who knew all about farming, commerce and medicine. His prayers resuscitated the dead; showing his victory over death. What manner of Man is this?

Though a civilian yet he ordered military commanders and even diseases. Lepers were cleansed, hemorrhoids disappeared, demons fled into herds of swines, and trees died at his command. He even ordered water to turn into wine, and it obeyed. He charged the storm to be still, and it acquiesced. He healed every patient who cried for healings and all manner of diseases. His compassion compelled him to heal every child that was brought to him and had compassion for widows that he raised up their children. What manner of Man is this?

He was a man of justice who forgave even those who hurt him. Ask Malchus; he replaced his ear that Peter severed in anger. He made outcasts insiders. What manner of Man is this?

He was a man with little education, but he spoke in parables witted in almost every figure of speech language could afford. Mud in his hands was eye medicine to heal the blind. He ordered fishes to pay his taxes so that Him and his followers would comply with human law too. If he was living in America, the IRS will be his bosom friend. What manner of Man is this?

He was a man that was rejected and despised by those who should have loved and honored him. He was betrayed by his own friend. He was acquainted with grief; a man of sorrow indeed! He was hated from birth and those who hated him finally killed him. He accepted the punishment just so He may impute righteousness on the sinful world. He understood people's sorrows and chagrins too. What manner of Man is this?

He is the only man whose dates of birth and death were already foretold before he was born. When his corpse touched the ground, dead people abandoned their tombs and came to town. He is the only dead who ever ascended into heaven so that you too may conquer death. God made him the only way to Him.

Give a shout out to Jeeeeeeeeeeeeeeesus Christ! Yes, Jesus Christ!

Until then, know Jesus and your sins will be forgiven.

Chapter Eighteen

Would you Sing 2012 Song In 2013?

The Israelites were taken into captivity in Babylon. They were frustrated: sadness and gloom had overtaken them. So they hung their music instruments on trees. But their captors wanted them to sing them a song: one of the songs of Zion (songs of freedom and gratitude). So they asked "how shall we sing the Lord's song in a strange land" (Psalm 137:4). Indeed it wasn't just a strange land but a land of mourning and torments because they were in captivity. So I ask you: why would you want to sing the song of 2012 that held you in captivity in 2013? If it was good; sing it, but if it was not why sing it in 2012?

We are just leaving 2011 and we are entering 2013, so we call it New Year. But though some say New Year, they are actually going to live the same old year over and over again. I know you are shaking your head saying huh huh; not me. Well, listen and listen well; many will transport and transfer their 2011 burdens into 2012 rather than let 2011 wash them away.

Are you still carrying enemies of 2011 to 2013? Please forgive them and move on. Perhaps there are many people who are repulsive and repugnant that you want to slap them every minute. Please forgive us going to New Year.

Are you still allowing the same creditors to pursue you into 2012? If not then endeavor to pay your debts. You made all the money from overtime, but your marriage went kaput and now you are singing the song of divorcees. You went late to all your appointments in 2011. Please don't carry that habit into 2013. New Year new fashion dear! You ignored everyone who could truly appreciate you but ran after those who regarded you as dirt. Well, "as you make your bed so shall you lie on it."

You always lose interest when someone else is telling you their problems, but you want others to memorize yours. You succeeded in killing your body pains, but the same painkillers did not work for your emotions. You drove the most comfortable cars but within you there was no comfort. You gulped sleeping pills yet married to insomnia. You attended stand up comedies and laughed, but after you left your trail of unhappiness sorrowfully pursued you to your home that you even contemplated suicide. How hopeless again did you want to be? Perhaps your parents made a mistake; they should have given you the middle name of Hopeless.

Last year you sang that you were overweight although you were just curvy. See Zakougla with her heavy duty body defying the little body theory. Body size does not matter for even midgets could entertain.

You were ignorant last year; could not even discuss the politics of your own very country talk less of other countries. Do you plan to go into 2013 again ignorant? You don't mean it; do you? Then sit down and read! Again I say unto you read!

Furthermore, let us say you have been sick now for long time and have been using western medicine, but your condition has not improved. Don't you think it could be time to try herbs? Sometimes I tell people that I think this herb, or this could cure you. They look at me in disbelieve. Or let us say you are always sick. Don't you think it is time to review your eating habits? See, if I have not been sick for 15 years today then there is something I am doing right in addition to God's healing, protection and preservation.

Those things you consider yours which the Lord cannot even touch; do not really belong to you. If he took away his breath you will be a smelling bunch after two days. I know some of us even stink while we are still alive so let me give it 5 days; you will be a smelling heap in 5 days. You smile; don't you?

You have too much time to play video games but no time to call and visit relatives. You played all you wanted, but the couch made you fat. Yes, you are obese! You have too much time to watch soap operas but no time to sit and read your bible. When was the last time you read your bible and actually knelt down to pray? Too much time for over time but no time to work on your marriage? Do you still think running around while married is in vogue? If you were even single, one could say you are testing the waters, but you have made a commitment to enter into a covenant my friend.

You have been a victim of infidelity. Take your life in your hands and don't go into 2013 singing the 2011 song.

For those who are single, you have created many accounts from different dating sides and you have attempted tryst by happenstance, you have sucked ambrosia from every straw and licked every lollipop to no avail. I mean you have inundated the dating side with your photos yet no pretender. You have compromised your values, but it only led you to pain and regrets. It means something was wrong somewhere somehow. You don't fix that which was not broken, but you must fix that which is not working. Albert Einstein once said: "insanity is doing the same thing over and over again and expecting different results." If those methods in 2012 did not work, do not take them into 2013, you will be merely transferring your pains and chagrins. Behold I bring you good news.

It is time to sit down and pray, read your bible, fast, and live for God. You compromised in 2012 but nothing did change, because God's must are not ifs. Those same friends you want to emulate can tell you they are miserable; miserable like the cockroach; vulnerable to everybody. "Delight thyself also in the LORD; and he shall give thee the desires of thine heart. Commit thy way unto the LORD; trust also in him; and he shall bring it to pass. I have been young, and now am old; yet have I not seen the righteous forsaken, nor his seed begging bread." (Psalm 37:4-5; 25). Let the lord be your Standard Bearer and lighthouse. If you follow God he will give you abundant life.

Until then, Happy New Year: I mean New Year not old in new.

Chapter Nineteen

Putting Up A Fight When The Devil Is Dragging You Down

Listen: this year has begun. Although we are determined to make it a better year, the devil is determined too to make it the worst year. So would you let him do it? A couple of my friends have confessed to me they no longer pray because they no longer trust God to do anything for them. If God was hearing their prayers, then He should have done something for them. Therefore, today I bring you good news. When Satan annoys you, don't let him have his way; get up, remove your sword in the spirit and fight till every captive including yourself is set free. God will surely come to your help. He does not fail, and He will never fail.

Listen: we had a Full Gospel Youth Camp in Mbamlayo. On the first three days it had rained, but usually while we were asleep. On Thursday, the rain began 30 minutes before we left the dormitory. My assistants whispered into my ears that we should suspend the evening campaign. Like Jannes and Jambres, they argued that the kids could catch cold and become sick. I looked at them and laughed. While they were sleeping I was praying in the night in the little bush by the side. So when the time reached for us to go, I told the kids that we will go into the rain and run with songs in our mouths until we reach the campaign grounds. While it was still raining, we prayed and I jumped into the rain, and I ordered the rest to follow me. As we began to run, two to five minutes later, the rain had stopped. On that day, one soul gave his life to Christ. Today, he is a pastor. When the devil is trying to drag you down please put up a fight. I say put up a fight!

Listen: it is disheartening how many times you have taken the same exam but have not passed. "For the eyes of the LORD run to and fro throughout the whole earth, to show himself strong in the behalf of them whose heart is perfect toward him."[1] I say study hard, pray, and go, and take it again. I don't care how long you have been sick, pray and believe God he is called Jehovah Rapha. The power of God has no comparison and those who believe in him will never be confounded.

Listen: don't allow the Devil to stab you again; you have a magic sword that you just need to hold, and it works magic for you. Use it. I say use it! It is true that your business has failed, and people are laughing at you. Don't allow the devil to stop you again. I say get up and fight. "Remember my brethren; be strong in the Lord, and in the power of his might. Put on the whole armor of God that ye may be able to stand against the wiles of the devil. For we wrestle not against flesh and blood, but against principalities, against powers, against the rulers of the darkness of this world, against spiritual wickedness in high places."[2] Are you giving up or you are putting up a fight?

Listen: before a soldier goes to war, he or she spends hours in training and practicing on hitting targets. Where do you train? Are you practicing to hit your targets? I say put up a fight. This year don't allow the Devil to push you around. Why are you a candidate for heaven, yet you allow yourself to be pushed around by a hell bound candidate? Look; you have allowed the devil to take you hostage; until you have lost hope: you are depressed. You have lost trust in God and you think he does not hear your prayers. You have tried by the arm of flesh but it did fail you. Look; the devil has given you a knock down, but I want you to rise up before the bell, and say though I am knocked down, but I am not knocked

---

1

2

out. I say put up a fight dear! The fire of the most high will consume your enemies as you put up a fight in prayer.

Listen: that private time you pray in your closet; that is your battle field. Don't allow the devil to bully around. God has not withheld good things from you; it's you yourself who has done that by listening to the devil that you cannot get them.

Listen: I know some of you are afraid to date again because every man that came, ran away like you are man repellant. I say, pray and start to date again. This time, put up a fight and tell the Devil "not this time again." Are you hearing me? Say not this time again! Anyone that is holding your answered prayers Angel Michael will be sent to liberate it as you battle in prayers. So I say get on your knees. Man, are you hearing me? Get on your knees; don't allow the devil to bully you again. Stop crying, get up and put up a fight. I want to see that face shinning with joy of inner peace. Sing the song of Zion my dear; it is the victor's song. Stop singing the song of Babylon; it is the song of defeat. I mean even if the devil gave you the name of Badluck that when you come to the door it closes in front of you. I know your husband is acting a fool like Nabal, and you have prayed, but the devil seems to be toying with you. I say get up, tell him not this around and pray again one more time.

Listen: do you remember when Elijah was praying for water? He sent Elisha to go and see if there were signs it was going to rain. He went and looked at it the first time but there was no sign of anything. Like them you have prayed the previous years but no sign of anything. He sent his servant again the second, third, fourth, fifth, sixth time and there was nothing. But the seventh time, he came back with an answer "Behold, there ariseth a little cloud out of the sea, like a man's hand."[3] Pray until you see your own little hand so that you can sing of your victory before you stop. Why are you not putting up a fight let your enemies be confounded.

3

Those who collude against you will themselves experience failure. Cry no more my dear; instead put up a fight for this is your year. Repeat after me: this is my year.

Until then, put up a fight when the devil is dragging you down.

Chapter Twenty

Where Is Your Destiny?

In whose hand is your destiny? Let me ask you this: who determines who you become? Humanists will tell you, you have your life in your hands. I tell you today; God has the whole world in his hands including your life. Listen to this anecdote.

A young woman worked for a company some years back. She worked with a boss who found pleasure sleeping with all the female workers under him. He employed only beautiful girls that he could later fool around with. Little did he know Nsosie would be different. He hired her and started his advances, but she turned him down. The more she turned him down, the more he gave her hell. Finally, with all the intrigues, the young woman was fired. The young woman tried to sue but failed with the collusion of other workers and her boss. She wept and cried before God. On their way back from a business trip, the boss' car veered off the road, and they all died. They did not live to enjoy the fruits of their intrigues. Such is a warning to those who plot against others.

Beware you who think the destiny of the weak belongs to you! To the weak who thinks his/her destiny belongs to the strong beware. God holds the whole world in his hands.

A neighbor was recommending a lawyer to me. I asked him how he knew the guy then he told me this story. He was Jewish, and he was African. Both were on a line to make their purchases when the white guy fell in front of him. Some were merely dialing their phones for 911, others were even unconcerned, but he rushed to the guy and placed him on his back and administered CPR; a thing he had only seen on TV. There were serious risks because if the man had died, he could have been charged, but he took the risk and revived the guy back to life before the ambulance could come. When the lawyer fully recovered, he got in contact with Ali. He later represented him in many cases for free.

If you are a human being, know that you do not hold the life of anyone; not even yours. God holds all our lives. Yes, say I am an ant, but no elephant can smash me. I am an elephant, but no hunter can shoot me down. Stop fretting when the wicked prosper. God will always defeat the devil and our enemies. Some of them pick up heart attacks and others are clawed by kidney disease. I lack the time for personal tales.

In 1988 in Douala was a brother in Christ who rented a house from a Duala man. The brother had paid them but because they wanted more money, they connived for their son to come and ask for rents again. The man complained that he had already paid their father, but they took his things and threw them out. The church prayed over it and told him that he should move out of the house. Neighbors said that is what that family did to rip people off. That brother moved out and rented another house. We could not help because we were a very small church, but God took control of the situation. An evangelist visited our church and rather than take offerings, he gave money to the family. Weeks later, the former landlord's youngest son fell in a well and died. The senior son died in an accident, and the third was going to France and got lost in the sea hitherto.

Didn't God tell you "Touch not mine anointed, and do my prophets no harm?"[4] Anyone with the seal of the Holy Spirit should know that "for he that toucheth you toucheth the apple of his eye."[5] Your destiny is in no man's hand my dear. Are your problems making you to be confused if God exists? Be no more, for He does! Stretch forth your staff and ask whatever red sea in your life to part and give you an escape route.

4

5

Until then, your destiny is in the hands of God.

Chapter Twenty-One

Are you a Simon of Cyrene?

When Jesus was on his passion to Golgotha, he fell on his knees. Because he was whipped and scourged, his strength was almost finished. If the guards let him there; then, he will not be crucified in time to beat the Sabbath. So in man's wisdom, they grasped Simon a Cyrenian whom they compelled to carry the cross of Jesus.

Simon was just coming from a trip when he met Jesus being led on the march to crucifixion. He had no business in it, yet he accepted willfully to carry the cross. There was a multitude behind Jesus, but no one volunteered to carry that cross. Instead, the women as usual bewailed and lamented for the son of Man; while, the men followed from afar in their usual cowardice.

Consequently, Jesus did not carry his cross alone; therefore, you cannot carry your cross alone. The easiest thing to do nowadays is to retreat into ourselves or become reclusive like hermits when trials and temptations lurk our paths. Stop carrying your cross alone!

The name Simon in Hebrews was given only to male children. It means "he who hears". I know that with the way the world functions today, it may look like no one is ready to hear your cries or feel your pain, but let me tell you this; this same Jesus who died on the cross that Simon carried, is ready to amortize your pain.

However, let me ask you reading me now, how many people have you helped to carry their crosses? How would you even carry their cross since you do not talk to strangers? Do you sit and watch people carry their cross to their death? Do you stand from afar to watch those who need your help plunge into suicide with their cross? Haven't you seen a friend who needs you to help them carry their cross? Don't you see a neighbor who needs your help in carrying their cross? You will start by knowing your neighbor first before you carry their cross. Don't you think so?

Listen: it is a shameful and wicked thing to be happy alone. You are leaving many people to carry their crosses alone. The Lord is telling you today it is wrong; not even Jesus who died for all mankind carried his cross alone. Someone helped him along the way. Would you be that someone to carry someone else's cross? Praise the Lord, then you are Simon the Cyrene.

Until then, help others to carry their cross.

Chapter Twenty-Two

Did You Murder Loyalty?

Nowadays, it is difficult to trust people. Ask most girls and they will tell you, "You cannot trust any guy." Ask guys and they will tell you, "You cannot trust any girl." Trust is lacking because people have killed loyalty. Underneath the word trust lies an ingredient called loyalty. There is no loyalty today. It is dead! Men and women cheat because they are not loyal. Friends betray friends because they are not loyal. As for others, they just don't know what is loyalty. Loyalty is a sign of true friendship.

Joseph of Arimathaea was a friend and disciple of Jesus. He was rich, but Jesus was poor. Yet that class disparity of material things did not keep them apart. One was spiritually rich while the other was materially rich. When Jesus died, him and another friend called Nicodemus still went boldly to Pilate (those who have killed their friend) to crave for his body knowing fully well he could be killed too. After all, those who called themselves his disciples had abduced and absconded into the oblivion; leaving the women to lament and wail. Pilate gave the corpse to them. They took it and wrapped it in a clean cloth, and then they buried it in his own new sepulcher which he had made for himself. I want you to learn a few things about loyalty and tell me if you are loyal. How many of us would risk our lives for our friend?

Years ago were two great friends who were loyal to each other. One of them owed the king some money, and he was supposed to pay it on a given date or die. His friend had a place where he thought he could go get the money to repay the king, but the king said he must bring a surety so in case he runs away; the surety would be his scapegoat. So his friend came and took his place in jail. Days passed, but he did not show up. The dateline was soon approaching. Minutes to the execution of his friend, he showed up to take his punishment because he could not get the money. The king decided to free both men. But before they left, the king asked the debtor's friend how he could trust his friend that he was going to come back. Wasn't him afraid of his life that his friend could abandon him there to skip town? He told the king that he has known him to be a loyal man.

Joseph of Arimathaea even gave his own sepulcher he had built for himself for Jesus to be buried in. He sacrificed the most precious thing he had for himself for his friend. Jesus to show us that loyalty to humanity, gave his life so that we may live.

How many of you out there are ready to sacrifice for your friend? Are you loyal to your friend when he or she cannot even call you at certain hours? You will tell them you are sleeping. Can your friend beg for a ride at late hours without you grumbling? Can you help your homeless friend with a place to live without it being the talk of the town? How are you loyal to your wife when you do not even want to better her life?

Joseph and Jesus complimented each other. Jesus brought spirituality to the table and Joseph brought money. Just because Joseph gave Jesus money, he did not try to make him his footstool. Some of us want to make our friends slaves once we give them anything. How loyal are you? True friendship must be engrafted with loyalty.

Until then, learn loyalty and let it live.

Chapter Twenty-Three

Are You Selling Your Birthright?

There is a story in the Bible about Esau: the eldest son who sold his birthright to his younger brother: Jacob. Birthright was the right given to the first born child whose mother was legally married, and was not a slave or concubine. It was for someone who normally would be the heir when his father passed away. The advantage was that he received a double portion of the property (Deut 21:7) and served as the family head (Gen 27:36). Women did not receive birthrights because families were patrilineal or considered paternally. Though the first born acquired the birthright status naturally by birth, it was also like a privilege that could be seized. That is why Reuben's own was taken away from him. Why didn't God give it to those after Reuben (Gen 25: 31-34)? Birthright could be taken away from you if you defiled it (I Chr 5:1). He defiled it by committing incest (Gen 49: 1-4). Their father bypassed them for lack of character and charisma (Gen 49:5-10). Instead, he gave it to Joseph his favorite son (Gen 49:22-26). Birthrights could be exchanged between the heirs and those who coveted it. That is why it was possible for Esau to give it to Jacob for some bread and portage of lentils. Once exchanged, it could not be taken back. But here is the crux.

> And Esau said unto his father, Hast thou but one blessing, my father? Bless me, even me also, O my father. And Esau lifted up his voice, and wept (Gen 27:38).

By selling that birthright, Esau showed he loved the world more than God; thereby making enmity with God, for the friend of the world is the enemy of God. That is why God hated Esau. Why could Isaac not take it back, or why couldn't he give another one to Esau if he could not take it back? He could have given him another one if it was just a physical thing. It was also a spiritual thing. Blessings were spiritual words and words uttered are irretrievable. Balaam said "How shall I curse, whom God hath not cursed, or how shall I defy whom the LORD hath not defied" (Num 23:8)? Isaac represented God and once he had blessed him to inherit the birthright, he could not recover it because there could only be one family head at a time.

The promise for him to be the heir was not through the law, but through the righteousness of faith since the just live by faith. Remember that "without faith it is impossible to please him: for he that cometh to God must believe that he is, and that he is a rewarder of them that diligently seek him." [6]Esau did not have the faith that God will carry him through the hunger. Do you have faith that God will carry you through your situation?

It is the writer to the Hebrews (12:16-17) who gives us a clearer picture of its significance. This passage exposes to us that even repentance and forgivingness will not erase the consequences of certain sins or mistake that we do. Verse 16 explains that just for the moment or the desire to satisfy the immediate desires of the flesh, people like Esau overlook long term consequences. That of Esau was the result of a bad decision, and there are consequences of certain bad decisions we must live with for life. He reacted to his immediate need not looking at the long term consequences. Take a look at unprotected sex or illicit sex as a whole. Just for the pleasure of the moment, many forgo their long term commitments and alliance and break the covenant of the marriage vows.

Spiritually, Jesus is the firstborn, and he takes the inheritance. Then we as his brothers and sisters become the coheirs (Rom 8: 29; Col 1:17-19; Heb 1:2-6). I pray that the eyes of your understanding would be enlightened so that you

6

may know the hope of His calling, and what the riches of the glory of His inheritance for the saints.

Until then, guard jealously your birthright.

Chapter Twenty-Four

Living The Talk

There is not a single week a former student or present student doesn't call, email or text me. I have been to court with some, and others I have visited in their sick beds. Most I have visited in their homes. Others I have looked for work, and some I have actually helped with cash and kind. Most remember I was strict, but at the same time I am caring and compassionate. For the past ten years, my disciplinary referrals are not up to a dozen. That is why they can sit back and differentiate between my being strict in class and my care and compassion for them out of class. It is good to talk about Jesus as the answer, but it is better to live Jesus as the answer. We may not be perfect, but we must strive for perfection.

A woman told me what the pastors and leaders of her church did to her, and it left me dumbfounded. Is that being the light of the world, and the salt of the earth? Treat people right, and they will follow your Jesus. Did you see any youth leave the mission while I was the leader? Now, look before I came and after I left. Listen to this: "let your light so shine before men so that they will see your good works and glorify your father who is in heaven".

Are we still taking strangers into our homes? I mean strangers: someone you do not know. Today people tell you how can I take someone in that I don't know? They say that you could be hurt. Whosoever shall seek to save his life shall lose it; and whosoever shall lose his life shall preserve it (Mt 17:33. I have always taken people in and though some have stolen from me, but the Lord replenished it. The Good Samaritan spirit is disappearing today.

A lady and her kids were stuck in a four way intersection. I went and parked by the side to try and push their car off the road. Motorists sat in their cars looking at me. Another one was honking. Two other people realizing I could not push the car by myself quickly joined me to push it off the road. I wanted to say a word to the lady honking at us, and as she passed me, I saw the fish sign on the back of her car. She is a Christian who cannot even step out of her car to help a helpless woman with kids. How many times have you stopped by to help anyone; I mean someone in trouble?

Sunday morning, I was going to preach in one church when I saw some four black older women by the road side looking bewildered. Their gas was finished. So I stopped by to help, and another brother I was giving a ride told me that, "brother you have to leave these things when you are with me. I don't want to go to church late". Which was more important: going to church on time or helping these daughters of God who were stuck by the roadside? I reminded him of the story of the Good Samaritan. We went and bought the gas and brought to the ladies. They were happy and blessed us as we both went to church. Nowadays there is a common saying that: "don't talk to strangers". Doesn't the bible say, "be not forgetful to entertain strangers for thereby some have entertained angels?"[7]

I carried a 55 year old white guy in the car, so we could go to the ATM for me to give him some money. After about a mile, he began sobbing. You know I am allergic to being quiet, so I then engaged him into a conversation. Then he told me that his wife ran away with a young man for 8 years. She came back and lived with them again for two years, and she just ran away again with another guy. He said "she is into that powder and crack stuff. She goes to the church down the street there". Going to church is not the issue; but living a life that is worthy of church going; a life that shows others you know God.

---

[7]. Hebrews 13:2

People, there is one thing I will like everyone to know. If some people cannot sleep because of what you do to them, you will not sleep yourself for fear of what they will do to you. That is why you see oppressors always look for better means to keep the oppressed oppressed because they are afraid of what they will do them. Treat people right and you will sleep in peace not fearing any reprisals.

Until then, live what you preach and teach!

Chapter Twenty-Five

Unapproved Workman

Just this week, I have had four Christians send me to read from an author to defend their point of view. Imagine someone standing in front of your door with a vacuum cleaner that they claim could work wonders. Then you ask them to teach you how it works. They tell you to instead go and read the handbook. That is exactly the way many Christians behave. When you ask them questions, they say go and read this book. What a travesty! I want us to look at a verse:

> *Study to show thyself approved unto God, a workman that needeth not to be ashamed, rightly dividing the word of truth.*[8]

God inherently encourages the laborer to study. It is true that too much learning brings too much sorrow (ECCL 12:12), but that is when we study to argue against futilities because those arguments are confusing, useless and destructive to an extent (2 Tim 2:14) especially when we spend our time studying myths and fables (I Tim 1:4).

To study means to give diligence. You cannot study without reading. It is true you may learn by listening, but you must read, and we must read the Bible. It is abnormal for a true Christian to be in the faith for 3 years, but they have never read the Bible from cover to cover while they have read Harry Potter and the tragedies of Shakespeare.

To show thyself means to be ready, to be there to help. To stand side by side that means to be able to carry a

---

[8] 2 Timothy 2:15.

debate. Don't take the pretext that the debate is meaningless to cover your nescience.

To be approved means to be acceptable or genuine. If you cannot defend what you believe in the bible, then you may appear like a counterfeit, or like a salesperson who does not know much about the merchandize they are selling. You are doing all of that for God (Unto God, so that the Godhead: (divinity) will approve you and prepare your crown on the day of reckoning. Faith comes by hearing and hearing the word of God. Some people used to tell me that it is not about knowing the Bible but putting it into practice. How would you practice something you don't know though? How would you become a good football player if you do not know the rules? You must learn the rules first. Because many Christians have failed to learn the rules of Christianity, they live as cousins of the devil.

You should be a workman who is not ashamed. Do not forget that when you give your life to Christ, you become God's laborer. So how would you work in a company you do not know the rules? You are a workman, but you want another person to read and tell you what the rules of the company say? How would you know your duties, rights and privileges?

My brethren, you are God's workmen. Take for example until you read Eph 6:10-19 you will not know how to fight the devil. Until you read Mark 9:29 you will not know how to cast out evil spirits. You will be an inefficient workman. And wouldn't you be ashamed if you are a Christian, but you can't even pray for a sick? I mean isn't it shameful if you are a Christian, but you do not know how to respect your father and mother?

The workman should be able to rightly divide the word of truth and to present the Bible objectively and honestly. What is this thing that we are preaching today, twisting the word of God to please the congregation? Someone is doing drugs and we think it is just their business and also their weakness. Then later we say everyone sins.

No, he or she should be rebuked. Tell them "your body is the temple of God. Whosoever destroys that temple he or she would be destroyed too".[9] The Bible wants us to present the truth objectively. Don't twist the bible or interpret the Bible to help your unbelief and hide the truth from the Christians. Show them the truth and the whole truth.

My appeal to you is to make a timetable to read the Bible everyday and at least three chapters. Try to memorize a verse every week at least. Listen; that is the only way you will be an approved workman of God who is not ashamed to rightly divide the word of truth.

Until then, may you be an approved God's laborer.

9

Chapter Twenty-Six

Never Give UP And Help Others To Never Give Up

I am sure you have watched the video, so I am going to make annotations on it. Derek Redmond was the favorite to win the 400 m race in the Olympics in Barcelona in 992 when a hamstring disaster struck. He could not continue the race, so he bent down and wept. Later he woke up and tried to finish the race. His father ran through the security to help his son. He tried to encourage him to stop running because he did not have anything to prove to anybody, but he said he had to finish the race. And together, they limped through the finish line on a standing ovation of the crowd.[10] This video reminded me of Moses, Aaron and Hur during the battle of Rephidim against the Amalekites. Moses had to intercede for Joshua to keep winning in the battlefield, but his hands were getting tired. So, Aaron and Hur took stones to support his hands (Ex 17:10-16). The Christian race is not looking for the first, but those who will complete the race. It is expedient that we help each other complete the race. Let me ask you this: are you ready to give up in life? Where is the dream you had? Who are you helping to finish the race of life? Ok now, I entreat you to learn from Derek Redmond.

The first thing we should learn from his situation is that none should ever boast himself/herself of tomorrow; for he/she does not know what a day may bring forth. On May 11, 2010, a Belmont couple who just celebrated their 45

10

anniversary died from a plane crash.[11] They did not know they will die on this day.

The second lesson we learn is that God is always by our side. He wants to help us if we can allow him to do that. He knows our chagrins and sees us cry in secret as in public. It depended on Redmond whether his father should help him or not. He put his head on his father's shoulder and cried. God wants you to trust him and cry on his shoulder. Why are you crying on shoulders that cannot help you? Cry on the one who began the race with you and who is ready to finish with you. God created you, and He knows your end.

Thirdly, we all are on a journey on earth. It is not who finishes first but who finishes the race at all. So if we are not going to win a trophy because we finish first, why are we jealous of one another? Why do we try to destroy each other? Why the schadenfreude? You must be your brother's keeper. Are you your sister's keeper? Will you be happy if you were left on this earth alone?

Finally, through his trial, we learn that all things work for the good of them that love the Lord. Redmond did not win the Olympic medal, but he had endorsements for endurance and for resistance. He became the epitome of resistance. He is even on a visa commercial. Even people who finished the race did not obtain the recompense he had. Derek Redmond taught us never to give up in life and to fight till the end. Today I encourage you to never give up and to encourage others to never give up.

11

Chapter Twenty-Seven

Do You Make Empty Pledges Just For Palmarès?

There are words that are intermittently and interchangeably used nowadays. Initially, a pledge was something you gave someone to hold till you sent your gift (Gen 38:17). Everything was accepted except human life (Deut 24:6). You were also not authorized to enter into someone's house to seize his pledge. The second is a vow. A vow was a votive offering you promised to give to someone towards a cause. For example, you can promise $1000 to a cultural organization towards their efforts to build a school. You could promise $100 to a church towards missions. However, the word vow is now commonly used as pledge although the real word we should be using is a vow. In a pledge, if you did not come back to fulfill your promise, the victim could keep your pledge but in a vow, you were dedicated to fulfill it (Num 30:2). While there was freedom in fulfilling a pledge, you were obliged to fulfill a vow because it was a debt! Nowadays the word pledge has replaced the word vow. For example: When you go to a cultural organization night and say you pledge $2000, you have committed yourself to make a votive offering (obligatory gift) because you are not giving them anything to keep till you bring your gift.

When I was writing this lesson, I remembered that I had made a pledge to one of my ex students. I had to go and fulfill it before I could post my lesson. The pledge you make is made unto God. It is not unto man though it is man who takes it. You are telling God to hold you by your words. Can we trust your words these days? I hear many girls tell me that you cannot trust a guy these days. The guys too say the same thing. Perhaps many do not know what a vow or pledge is. Let me show you examples of people who made such vows and how they fulfilled them. Solomon said God has no pleasure in fools, so if you make a vow fulfill it. (Eccl 5:4). It is better you do not vow than that you vow but do not pay (Eccl 5:5).

Let me put this into perspective. There are marriage vows, love vows, ceremonial vows (pledges) and many others. When a man and a woman promise to marry each other till death do them part, that is a vow they have made to each other. When you tell someone that I love you and will never leave you, that is a votive offering you have made. When you promise your daughter that if you pass the graduation test, I will buy you a laptop, you have just committed yourself to a pledge. If you promised to give $50 to a cultural group during their convention, that is a pledge. If you promised a church to give them $10,000 for the construction of church building, that is a pledge. Or perhaps you pledge to support the Cancer Society with a $10 a month donation. Such a promise was not a habitual or common promise or practice you made everyday. It was also not a promise you made or took lightly. If you pledged, you must fulfill it (Deut 23:21). If you know you will not do something, do not say it. Do not promise it! The only time you could not fulfill a vow (pledge) was if you died (Deut 23:22). A vow was the same as a written contract: it was not to be broken no matter how foolish it was.

For sample, if you promised a group $100 because you wanted to amaze a girl sitting on the other end that you are rich, you were obliged to pay the vow. If you made a vow during a fundraising party to give $500, you are obliged to pay your vow. It is not if but just when, but you must pay it. Sometimes you hear people who go to fundraising parties and pledge $1000 here and $1000 there but just to boost their palmarès, and they do not pay. Know that it is a sin before God and actually it brings you a curse. That is because the person who always breaks his promise brings a curse to himself/herself. If you know you cannot fulfill a pledge then don't do it. No matter how people coerce you and flatter you with titles, don't do it if you will not fulfill it. Sew your coat according to your size.

I went to one party, and they called me to sit with the other dignitaries. I knew I did not have money and did not want to make a pledge. So I refused going to the "High Table." They begged and promised me that they were not going to call me for money. I said, "man, I don't believe it. I am sitting down here. I am just fine." I knew that sitting on the High Table comes with donation or pledges (vow), and I was not ready for any.

Perhaps they are building a church somewhere, and the pastor is asking you all to promise how much you will give. If you know you do not have money, there is no reason to pledge. God knows you cannot give what you don't have, but if you decide to make a pledge just to please the pastor and the Christians, you must pay the pledge. The church has the right to ask you the money as a debt. There is a very sad and moving story of a man who kept his words.

Chapter Twenty-Eight: Jephthah: When the rejects becomes the precious. Jephthah's father got him from wedlock with a harlot. His step brothers and step-mother drove him away from their house. But when they were attacked by the Ammonites, they went and solicited his help. He asked them to make him their leader first before he could fight for them. They accepted and did according to his wishes. Then he in turn made a vow to God that if he won the war, he will give to God the first thing that came out of his house to greet him. Jephthah had only one daughter and the only child.

In those days, when someone opened the door, they first sent out the sheep and cattle. But on that faithful day, when Jephthah came, rather than the cattle, it was the daughter who was the first person to step out. The excitement to see the father had made her to forget ushering the sheep out first. Rather than joy, it brought him sorrow as the Bible says "when he saw her, that he rent his clothes, and said, Alas, my daughter! thou hast brought me very low, and thou art one of them that trouble me: for I have opened my mouth unto the LORD, and I cannot go back". She told her father to carry his vow but to give her two months to bewail her virginity. After two months, she came back, and her father sacrificed her to fulfill his vow. Though it was foolish, but he had to do it.

Hannah was another example who promised God that if God gave her a child, she will give Him back the child to serve him as a priest. That is how and why Samuel became a priest (I Sam 1:11; 21).

So let me ask you this. Have you made a pledge anywhere? Did you pay it? You must pay it. If anyone made a pledge to an association, their names should be written in the book of debtors and they should be required to pay the money with every debt collection procedure followed.

Until then, pay your pledges for they are debts.

Chapter Twenty-Nine

Knocked Down But Not Knocked Out!

In September 24, 2005, Samuel Peter of Nigeria was fighting the Ukrainian- Wladimir Klitschko for a 12 round elimination match. After 4 dull rounds, Peter knocked down Klitschko twice in the 5th round. Peter gave the crowd the momentum and created belief for himself. The crowd chanted Peter, Peter, Peter and waited eagerly for the greatest upset that did not come. To add more impetus, Peter knocked Klitschko down again in the 10th round. He stalked and chased him across the ring looking for the killer punch that will finish his opponent. To many, it was just a matter of time before Peter knocks out Klitschko. However, to the chagrin of spectators and the frustration of Peter, Klitschko picked himself up, slugged and outpointed Peter (who began gasping for air) to a unanimous decision. Just because you are knocked down doesn't mean you are knocked out!

Only death brings the end of hope. As long as we are alive, let us have hope that God does not fail and will not fail. He may not walk with the pace of a man because he is never in a hurry, but He is never late. Keep trusting Jesus he will never fail you. Life always serves us with a plate we did not order. However, let us not worry; we should only know the Cook is our very own Father Jesus whose meal will bless our hearts.

Fear sometimes cripples us but let faith moves us to higher bounds. Look around you, that is not how you began. You are not what you want to be, but thank God, you are not what you used to be. Just as every tunnel has a beginning, there is an end. Our dark days may be long and dreary but stay focus, your ray of light just proves you are winning. You will make it.

There are many in heaven looking down and hoping you make it too. Would you fail them? You owe them the responsibility of making it and seeing Father Abraham, Moses, Joshua, Gideon, Deborah, Esther, Daniel, John the Baptist, Paul, Apollos and finally Jesus.

My Brethren, the days keep getting darker and darker, and evil seems enveloping us all. You may be cast down but don't be downcast. If you do not want vultures to eat you, then don't die in an open field! Tell them that though you are knocked down, you are not knocked out. Show them that you are still in the ring, for it is not who wins but who can put up a fight till the Master comes. Do not care how fast the other is running; just stay focus on your direction. When you stumble, lift yourself up and keep running knowing that it is not a race to find the first but finishers.

I have made up my mind to leave the world behind me, take up my full armor to face the tides of life that try to beat me round. At times I crawl with tears in my eyes, other time I run with joy in my heart. I may not be walking or running but know that, in so far as I am not standing, I am on the move. Sometimes during your down moments, even your phone calls will become like a disease that people run away from. Don't worry; make one to Jesus, for he always picks the calls of friends when they need him most. More so, He does not complain what time is this. He tell you "coheir, I am on my way. Just a little bit of patience".

That at once illumines and brightens my day because while on earth, the sister of IRS loved him as he even paid his taxes from the mouth of a fish. His legs were his car and now that gas prices are hiking, he will be treading on familiar territory. Everywhere he visited, he was doing good. Some people did not need to buy medication, for He used just mud to heal their blindness. He prepared a meal in the presence of foes and friends alike and their baskets were overfilled in a football field. Just with two loaves and five fish he will feed more than ten thousand.

Look at you with teary face. Why are you crying when you can make that early phone call? You think your situation is hopeless, and life is not fair. True, life is hopeless and unfair without a chemistry with Jesus. Seest thou not that thy Lord lovest thee that much my brethren? Why lookest thou unto thyself when thy Hope beckoneth.

Your Master, though gone is always around you. You know He loves you very much. When the devil tries to push you over, you over push him in prayers. When trials and temptations come over you in their myriads, you be the overcomer the Lord has smoothened. Say to yourself, I came to this world not of my choice but of his own likeness. I was made more than a conqueror without a vote, I shall live as a conqueror in the midst of warriors and shall die a conqueror even if all others are killed. Lord unto you I surrender my life.

Until then, even though you are knocked down, you are not knocked out.

Chapter Thirty

Jephthah: Despised But Not Useless

Do you look at yourself with great talents and skills, yet you are unable to place food on your table? You were due for promotion, but your company bypassed you and compounded your misery with letting you go. You sing like an angel and dance like a cock, but no producer has accepted your works. You write like Shakespeare and John Donne, but publishers reject your works. Many doors keep closing right in front of your nose. Before I tell you today's story, I want to remind you about our contemporaries. After many rejections, in 2007, lady Gaga was in her "tiny apartment praying God that someone will believe in her", and Akon finally believed in her when no one would. Today you know who she is. "Clinton charity foundation began 10 years ago in 2001 as a one man foundation, but today many follow the dream." In this lesson, you will learn that simply because you are rejected, you are not useless because no mortal can dispossess you of the dream that God has destined for you if you stay steadfast to harness your skills knowing that your hardship was a hibernation period. So today I will tell you the story of Jephthah: a man who was despised and rejected but later became the judge (ruler) of the entire Israel.

Jephthah means he opens. Him that God sets free or open to go. He was the son of Gilead and a concubine. He was conceived out of wedlock, but he was a mighty man of valor, a brave soldier. Jephthah was strong physical because faith then was lived physically. Can we call you a mighty person of valor. To be strong spiritually, you must adorn thyself with the weapons of warfare in Eph 6: 10-18. His father Gilead got married and had other children. After Gilead died, Jephthah's step brothers and sisters decided to thrust him out because his mother was not married to their father when he was conceived.

They were acting according to the guidelines of inheritance that existed in those days. Children out of wedlock did not have birthrights. Rather than stay back and fight, he decided to leave because he knew the laws and people of the land were against him (V.7) and also because he trusted God. This passage does not say so, but we know so because the writer to the Hebrews registered him amongst the men of faith (Heb 11:32). After his brethren drove him, he went and joined other worthless men in Tob (a nearby city), and they formed a band where he was the leader. Take note of Matthew 21:42.

As time passed, Israel was attacked by Ammon because they accused Israel for seizing their land when she was coming out of Egypt, passing through Arnon, Jabbok, unto Jordan. So the elders (leaders) of Gilead went to look for Jephthah to come and fight for them. Do not think that those who despise you do not know your importance; they are merely jealous and unsecured. When they solicited his help to lead them into war to fight the Ammonites, he told them to remember that they had driven him before and now they need his help. Those who hurt you will come to you for help.

The elders told him that it is true they had hated and driven him but now they have come back to their sense and they need him. If a people do not want you to lead them, let them be; when the time comes that they need you, they will come for you. Never force yourself on anyone who does not want to deal with you. Jephthah would be made the judge of Gilead and Israel. The elders even made a vow that he would be their leader. God knows how to prepare a table before you in the presence of your enemies and your cup runs over. However, the realization of this dream does not come without sacrifice.

That is why the Bible says "And Jephthah vowed a vow unto the LORD, and said, If thou shalt without fail deliver the children of Ammon into mine hands, Then it shall be, that whatsoever cometh forth of the doors of my house to meet me, when I return in peace from the children of Ammon, shall surely be the LORD'S, and I will offer it up for a burnt offering." Jephthah won his battle as God kept his side of the bargain. It was now time for Jephthah to keep his. He has made a very strange vow to God; that he would sacrifice the first thing that came out of his house. It is a very strange vow that he was making because of the outcome.

At this time it always the custom of women to go and receive the warriors with timbrels and dances as they were entering into the city. That is why you will see the women do it to David when he killed Goliath (I Sam 18:6).

Yet, it comes as a surprise to Jephthah that the first thing to appear out of his house was not a cattle it was his only daughter. Just to situate you why he was expecting something else other than his daughter. In those days, people slept in the same house with their cattle. When it was dawn, the rearer opened the door and put out the stronger and older sheep first so they do not overrun the younger and weaker ones. So Jephthah knew that if anything was to come out of his house, it would be a cattle but even if it was the fattest cattle that came out, he was ready to sacrifice it.

Many people will despise you in times of your failure or weakness, but in your days of greatness and fame, they will want to identify themselves with you. It is failure that is an orphan; success always has relatives and extended relatives. Some people will say I did not know you were going through what you are going now. If I knew, I would have helped you. That is what the Ephraimites were saying; I mean the same people that Jephthah invited them to give him a helping hand but they ignored him (Judges 12:1-2). He finally judged Israel for six years, and he died and was buried in Gilead; the land he was previously driven from.

People have always asked me why God would accept the sacrifice of Jephthah's daughter. Jephthah had made a non redeemable vow because he had selected the vow of devotement. It means his daughter was to be devoted for the services of God as a temple virgin. It is clear that the sacrifice that Jephthah meant there was not the same as the Baal worshippers did by killing people they offered to Baal.

In Israel, there were two types of vows: redeemable vows and non redeemable vows. To redeem a vow you could not fulfill, you paid money. If you did not have money, you saw the priest to offer yourself. It is not that Jephthah killed his daughter but that he had to give his daughter for the services of God as such, she will never get married. Consequently, Jephthah would not have any other children (Judge 11:) and his lineage will get extinct. She was to remain a temple virgin.

At first we see that Jephthah's daughter did not just follow her father, but she also believed and feared God that is why she told him that "My father, *if* thou hast opened thy mouth unto the LORD, do to me according to that which hath proceeded out of thy mouth; forasmuch as the LORD hath taken vengeance for thee of thine enemies, *even* of the children of Ammon." (Judges 11:36). This was a girl with a living syneidesis and a father with a high synteresis. Verse 37 gives us a clearer picture of the nature of sacrifice he was to sacrifice. If she was to be killed, she would not wail for her virginity.

Because she was going to be a temple virgin, it was her whole life spent in the temple; whereas, she had not enjoyed the reason for which she kept herself a virgin. Verse 39 again even paints the picture pellucidly when it says that her father did with her according as he had vowed and she knew no man. Therefore, her father gave her to the temple as a result the young girls of Israel went to lament with her for 4 years every year.

My friend, let those who think you are a nobody and have no skills keep sleeping on the first bench, but you know what you have. Paul had been rejected though the great skills, but Barnabas believed in him. One day someone will surely believe in you. You know what you are made of.

Nurture and harness your skills waiting for that golden opportunity. Fight and leave no stone unturned until you find the milieu where you will exercise your great talents. Jesus will fight your secret battles in your great time of need. Would you like for me to ask you if you have ever believed in anyone and given them the opportunity at their time of need?

Until then, just because you are despised does not mean you are useless.

Chapter Thirty- One

The Inspirational Testimony of Chuck Smith

This video link was given to me by a friend from Germany: Erik Erstfeld. Since he gave it to me, I have listened to it thrice. If you grew up a Christian and have had time to read the Bible for yourself then you will agree with the testimony of Pastor Chuck Smith of the Calvary Chapel. If you have read it and are wondering why the church is nowadays a tinkling cymbal, you will have to listen to the testimony. The testimony challenges your faith, demystifies the myth that one must know their partner for years before they marry, and it also shows you the failure of the church with institutionalized religion and denominational attachments. That is because it is "Not by might, nor by power, but by my spirit, saith the LORD of hosts."

I know the God we serve is not only for Elijah, Peter or Paul to raise up the dead because as a young Christian, my niece was brought back to life, and that made my family to surrender their lives to Jesus.

Nowadays there are many who believe that they must know someone for years before they marry them. Chuck Smith had 6 weeks of courtship and engagement before they got married; meanwhile, they had never known each other before. We cannot know anyone! Despite many trying out partners for soul mates. Yet him and the wife live a happy matrimony though married for more than 20 years.

In the video, one will learn that, the more spiritual you become, the less denominational you become. Churches and Christians are so clawed today on denomination that they look at each other with suspicion and even hinder the work of Jesus in quest for denominational superiority. Weak churches and pastors are always threatened by seeing another servant of God. Rituals and institutionalization is what sets in most groups when the spirit has left a group of Christians.

Him and his wife lived by faith. If they prayed and something did not happened, they knew that is the way God wanted it, and they did not fret. The person who knew how to manage the money handled the money. It was not a thing where every spouse wants their independence. One of the causes of divorce in the western world is finance. If you live by faith, you will live a simple life style and believe that God will provide. Never did you hear them say they need money and that without your financial contribution this ministry will not continue. Ok, let it not continue, for it is not your work; it is the work of God. When a pastor starts to feel like to showcase his or her worldly success, one can know that their hearts are not in sync with the spirit.

His bible school teachers influenced him with their expository teachings. Expository teaching is the key to proper teaching. Do you wonder why Christians nowadays cannot even pray, do not know how to pray and are ignorant of the promises of God in the Bible for them? That is the reason why feel good preaching has invaded and taken modern Christianity hostage. This is one of the causes of the backward degradation of godliness in America. Why is Bible study attendance today scanty and boring? That is because Bible studies nowadays are no more conversational and apologetic but religious façades or monologues.

Today people try to raise bodyguards rather than disciples. When you raise disciples, their sole focus is to be like Jesus Christ. He requested for outward change first and that the physical will follow later. Those changes can only come when the Christian becomes prayerful and full of the word. There are Christians that have never read their bibles from Genesis to Revelation, and there are Christians who spend a day without praying for at least one hour. How are they expecting transformation? How are they expecting their faith to grow since faith comes by hearing and hearing the word of God? Transformation comes by going closer to God, and we get closer to God by prayers my dear!

Ministry is for the anointed and well equipped teachers who have died to self and have nothing to protect. Men do not need to be degreed to be efficient ministers but must be called to ministry, and they prove that in the way they do the ministry. Look at people like Jonathan Edwards, George Muller, John Knox they did not have those big degrees, but they affected their contemporaries more that the big doctors of today whose lives have never and would not even affect a dead fly. Chuck did not believe that people needed education to be in the ministry, but you need to go into the ministry and learn in it. Indeed, he is a great man of God to emulate!

Until then, seek your revival.

Chapter Thirty- Two

Good Name: Killed By Money and Fame

Not every famous person is rich but we could say every rich person is famous. Role models overnight and little messiahs within their communities. Their private lives are the open records of paparazzi and the sinful public elevating them to moral gurus. After all, "money talks louder than the truth". The rich and famous are known by all for their money buys them admirers; their living is made easier by their riches as they live in opulence.

But here is another side you did not know about the rich and famous. Most of them live in fear of the unknown, are wicked: pilfering even from the poor as you saw in WorldCom and Enron. They pretend to care but they don't care about justice, and strive on taking advantageas confessed by Kanye West. They fancy gathering with other wicked people as Hollywood can show. Their inner insecurities lead them to plastic surgery, murder, hate and destruction. If fame and money would make us happy then stars would not be drug addicts? When the joy within escapes an individual then a replacement is sort through addiction. One would understand that the poor wants to drown their sorrows but what about the one you envy? If Oprah picks up weight it means her Acai Berry Diet does not work. So why do you want to follow processes that do not work?

Why is 419 instead taking another dimension? People regard fame and money more than good name. People even ask you if we eat good name. Despite news that the world oldest profession is feeling the crisis young women are still freighting into the business. Some may be fighting for survival but many want money and fame. In 1990 Richard Lyon killed Nancy Dillard for money." Dominick Dunne's "Power, Privilege and Justice" leaves you glued to your seat as you watch the debasement of human morals. The desire to acquire money has led many into vaulting ambitions that overleapt their bounds. Nowadays people are judged by virtue of their riches rather than the riches of their virtue. Consequently, good name is slaughtered on the altar of fame and money.

The Bible says that the love of money is the root of all evil (I Tim 6:10). In our attempt to be rich and famous, we fall into temptation and foolish lusts which drown us into destruction and perdition. Many have so coveted after money that they have erred from the faith and pierced themselves through many sorrows.

Can we find people today who will return lost goods? In Ljubljana: capital of Slovenia out of 30 lost cell phones 29 were returned to their owners . In Africa, America and Latin America out of 30 cell phones kept to the view of adults; even children, will be stolen. Thereby killing good name for fame.

The Bible puts wisdom on a higher pedestal to money (Eccl 7:12) because wisdom strengthens the wise than ten mighty men in the city (Eccl 7:19). But the world is the opposite. It went further to say that though wisdom is better than all the weapons of war one sinner destroys all good (Eccl 9:18). So sinners beware! Surprisingly, the world does not heed to the poor man's wisdom (Eccl 9: 16). That is why the rich stars are now the sages of the society, even the vilest of them is a role model. .

Make no mistake the Bible says that money answers all (Eccl 10:19). But you and I know money does not answer all childlessness, ill health and stupidity. No man has two penises and no woman has three vaginas. Worst still both have only 24 hours a day. You can get drudged in all the leisure and pleasure but you will end up mocking and destroying yourself.

Therefore, that verse does not mean that when you are rich your problems are packed in a suitcase and thrown into the Pacific Ocean. You may drink all the wine you can, eat all the goodies you can afford, or do all the drugs you find but without wisdom you are a miserable being. Wisdom is the fear of the Lord.

If you want to laugh without and still laugh within choose wisdom. Wisdom will bring you good name too. But you will never know both wisdom and evil. This is one of those times where the law of Exclusive Middle works at its best. Madness and folly cannot be married to wisdom. We live as a shadow on earth and we do not even know what will happen to the fame and money we leave behind. All we are entitled to is eat and drink for that is what will abide with us all of our life because we were created to fear God and keep his commandments and not to run after fame and money. So why do we pursue things that do not satisfy our souls? Have you ever sat to reconsider the emptiness of the life we live trying to run after fame and money while those with fame and money are married to sleeping pills?

People with good name will be remembered but the name of the wicked shall rot.

Doesn't the Bible say: a good name is rather to be chosen than great riches, and loving favour rather than silver and gold (Prov 22:1)? Solomon the wisest man did emphasize: a good name is better than precious ointment; and the day of death than the day of one's birth (Eccl 7:1).

Until then, may we resurrect good name back.

Chapter Thirty- Three

How to know you are still a Christian.

1. When you do not sell your birthright for pottage
2. When you "do not tempt the Lord thy God".
3. When you worship and serve only the Lord your God.
4. When you repent of your sins.
5. When you fish for lost souls.
6. When you are meek.
7. When you hunger and thirst after righteousness.
8. When you are merciful.
9. When you are the pure in heart.
10. When you are persecuted for righteousness' sake.
11. When they persecute you for Christ's sake.
12. When you act like the salt of the earth and the light of the world.
13. When you do not break nor teach others to break the commandments of God.
14. When your righteousness exceeds that of the Pharisees.
15. When you do not feel comfortable in sin.
16. When you forgive those who offend you.
17. When you love thy neighbor.

18. When you love your enemies, bless them that curse you, do good to them that hate you, and pray for them which despitefully use you, and persecute you.

19. When you greet even people you do not know.

20. When your tithes and offerings are not to show off.

21. When you have a personal time of prayer.

22. When you fast.

23. When you do not live for materials things.

24. When rather WORRY for future, you trust God.

25. When you do not judge with partiality.

26. When you discern false prophets.

27. When you do not teach things you do not do.

28. When you do not flatter people.

29. When you do not always seek to rule others.

30. When you fight for marginalized.

31. When you do not only show your righteousness in public.

32. When you do not only respect portions of the Bible that support your behavior.

33. When you like to assemble with other Christians.

Until then, let the Christians act Christian and the world will be transformed.

Chapter Thirty-four

The Lord Is MY Shepherd: What It Truly Means

Every Christian can tell you something about the verse the "Lord is my shepherd I shall not want". My task today is to create a mental picture of this verse. I will start by defining two words: "shall" and "want" that will be capital in the development of our lesson. "Shall" in legal settings general denotes mandatory and imperative action. The word "want" as used in this passage means lack. It is synonymous to the word need and not want in economics. In other words; the verse should read and mean this "the Lord is my shepherd, and I will never lack the necessities". This theory is sustained by Paul's letter to the Philippians "But my God shall supply all your NEED according to his riches in glory by Christ Jesus" (Philippians 4:19). The psalmist goes further to sustain his declaration by saying "I have been young, and *now* am old; yet have I not seen the righteous forsaken, nor his seed begging bread" (Psalm 37:25). However, there seems to be a conflict between prescription and description because we see fervent Christians lacking what we consider the basics amenities of life. If not does every Christian have everything they need? Why not?

If God was going to provide for everything we need then Jesus would not have said that "Man shall not live by bread alone, but by every word that proceedeth out of the mouth of God"(Mt 4:4). This is because Jesus came more for the spiritual man with whom he will build the spiritual kingdom. Even the most righteous person on this earth does not receive all their wishes or have everything they wish for. As a result, the Christian must know that their spirit will always be fed even if their body is hungry. Actually at times in fasting, the spirit is fortified ready for spiritual warfare than when the body is strong and well-fed. If God was to provide everything we need then he would not have asked us to pray for our daily bread.

Many Christians have taken this verse to mean that everything they want, they will receive and whatever they name and claim, they will receive. This has resulted in a lot of frustration from discouragement to total backsliding of the faithful. Walk with me gradually as I take the pain to start painting the image I promised you earlier.

When a shepherd has his sheep, he looks for green grass. In search of greener pastures many Christians moved to the US. Would anyone tell me if the most spiritual of them receives everything they ask from God? He knows where the grass is green and knows where we can find food if there is nothing around us. Many do not count on God for their provisions. They believe in their strength though they are Christians. God has only good plans for us. The shepherd does not always provide his sheep with immediate food. At times they have to walk for long to find food. During this time that they are walking like that, they are feeling very sad and dejected. It is the same with humans.

As I was growing up, shepherds took their cattle and trekked from Kousseri to Mamfe (587 miles) to sell them. During their journey, the shepherd took their sheep where they could eat and drink water. At times they came to cities that did not have anything for the cattle to eat and drink. The sheep will be going through this period of trial and perseverance until they came to a place where they could find something to eat.

One thing we must note is that the Lord will always provide our basic needs. But if he does not do it, He will know how to make us navigate through the dearth or scarcity. Always count on God for whatever you need. He knows best the things that are best for you. The Lord has lived your future, so he knows about it than you know anything about it. If you make him your shepherd, he will help you go through scarcity with joy. So let me ask you this: who is your shepherd? Are you counting on human beings? They will fail you.

Until then, make the Lord your shepherd and you shall not want.

Chapter Thirty- five

Hasn't God Forgotten You Peradventure?

As we look at the world and the happenings, we may think that God has gone on leave or vacation and has left human beings to struggle for themselves. The rich pilfer from the poor, and the oppressors think it is their God-given rights to oppress the weak. Stronger nations like the US, Britain, and France are invading weaker nations like Ivory Coast and Libya to siphon their natural resources. Those that made money their almighty purveyor soon realize it can only provide quasi happiness as they become aware of many millionaires suffering from insomnia. Despite the lauds and vespers of many not to lose their houses, the bank still foreclosed on them. Some named and claimed a happy marriage, yet it fell apart like a sandcastle. Others have been unemployed now for so long that if they were even renamed Unemployment as their middle name; it will be a befitting favor. Some neither have health nor death insurance but sickness strolls around their corridor. You are a beautiful girl, but sex that others crave and rave has become a nightmare to you because of pain here and pain there. It seems like your children have signed a pact with delinquency that immurement seems to beckon with both hands. You have written love letters that even Hera would have fallen, but the girl you lust and fantasize about has never given you a single reply. You are wondering if God has forgotten you.

Some are trying and relying on coping mechanisms like sex, drugs, alcohol, and social media to deal with this puzzlement so much so that many have become addicted. Others are in total denial, while some rationalize their misery and calamity. The young and old nowadays rather than run to God instead run to religion as another coping mechanism. The majority are drowning themselves in hedonism and embracing fatalism and existentialism body and soul. The tough subscribe to stoicism which reborn more hopelessness that suicide has increased than decrease.

Even great men of God like David (Ps 106:4) and Jeremiah (Jer 15:15) had thought at one point that God had forgotten them. It would seem the present generation is a generation that could rightly be called mobile drug depots of prescription and off counter medications. Even though the sex industry is also experiencing the recession, young girls are flooding into easy money stripteasing as their imaginary bliss terminus where they make a few bucks from spreading their legs to expose their sacred assets to lustful men; single or married. Yes, that is because most of them think God and human beings have forgotten them. Some of you know people who really do not want to see you. You fear for your life day and night. You sleep and keep an eye open that even a mere mosquito frightens you. Some of you have been so evil that even your own shadow frightens you too. Whatever may be the danger facing you, I want you to remember that God does not forget his people.

I know you have been praying, but today I tell you to garnish your prayers with faith in God. Go down again and pray a birthing prayer (I Kings 18: 42). I am not talking about going to church; I am talking about taking your cares unto God who cares for you. Faith and prayer will never fail you as they never failed Elijah. He prayed and asked his servant to see if the results were there. Rather than give up if there were no results, he went down back again and kept praying. Jesus said "men ought always to pray, and not to faint" (Lk 18:1), and Paul reiterated "pray without ceasing" (I Thes 5:17). Why are you ceasing to pray when your trouble is still there? Is it because you think God has forgotten you? Yes, Elijah prayed until God gave a mighty rain (I Kings 18: 42-46). Therefore, if you want an answer to your situation, hear me well; God has not forgotten you. No, he does not forget his own people "For the eyes of the LORD run to and fro throughout the whole earth, to show himself strong in the behalf of *them* whose heart *is* perfect toward him." (2 Chro 16:9).

Until then, wait patiently a little longer for God has not forgotten you!

Chapter Thirty- Six

Where Are All God's Watchmen and Watchwomen?

Are there still watchmen and watchwomen? Why is the destruction of the family so high? How come people are so alienated from God, addicted to technology, environmentally destructive? Can we explain the invasion of individualism and subsequent loss of community life? Why are there too many slaves to debts and consumerism? The rich ruling the masses? How come the neglect of children and maltreatment of women and men more common nowadays? Where are the watchmen and watchwomen when the media that was the source of truth now is the corrupt box of lies? Why does this seem the age where there is total neglect of the old and sick? The watchman was to look out against danger, foreign invaders. He was to spy, observe and watch at the city. As the watchmen were never to keep silent about impending danger, those that have been called by the lord to denounce evil and bring people to Christ cannot be silent (Isaiah:62:6-7). The task of the watchman and women nowadays.

So let me ask you this as a Christian who have you warned since you became a Christian. Do you know an adulterer and yet you have stayed mum? Do you know those who are openly living in sin, but you believe that is their lifestyle or alternative lifestyle? Do you know a known drug dealer or anyone who is doing drugs but you have decided to keep quiet because it is not your business? What about the scammer you hang out with? If that person dies, God will hold you accountable. Do you know a preacher who is pilfering from the church and the rich who are stealing from the poor, yet you think it is their problem and not yours? Do you have a father or mother who is a racist, but you refuse to warn them because you think how they want to live their lives is not your business? Hear me and hear me well; God holds you responsible if you know it but do not warn them. Perhaps, this is only the Old Testament. So what does the New Testament say about it too?

There are several passages in the Bible where the Bible is commissioned to preach the gospel to every creature (Mt 28:18-20), but the reaction to the gospel and the reaction of the preachers is what I will discuss here. I will start with the commission to Ezekiel. God tells him to act as a sentinel, warn both the wicked and the righteous. If the wicked abandons his wicked ways and returns unto the Lord, he will be saved, but if he does not, when he dies, his blood will be in his own hands. However, if the sentinel (Ezekiel) does not warn him, when he dies, God will hold Ezekiel responsible. Why was he to warn the righteous too? If verse 24 establishes this "But when the righteous turneth away from his righteousness, and committeth iniquity, and doeth according to all the abominations that the wicked man doeth, shall he live? All his righteousness that he hath done shall not be mentioned: in his trespass that he hath trespassed, and in his sin that he hath sinned, in them shall he die. " So the assignment here is very precise. Preach and warn the wayward of their waywardness. Whatever they do with that warning is their problem and not yours; you have fulfilled your responsibility. You can hear God through the mouth of Jeremiah rebuking the Israelites that "Thus saith the LORD, Stand ye in the ways, and see, and ask for the old paths, where is the good way, and walk therein, and ye shall find rest for your souls. But they said, We will not walk therein (Jeremiah:6:16)."

The first person to overtly repeat such a stand was Jesus. Although John The Baptist practiced it, but he did not preach it. John preached to those who wanted to listen and left those who did not. He even packed and went into the desert to live so that only those who wanted to really listen to him heard him. Simply because you warn people of their evil does not mean they will listen. However, when Jesus came, the story was different. He established three basic truths about the watchman. When you go out to preach, live with someone you know and don't change houses. Preach to those who want to listen and those who do not, leave them alone and go your way. God will take it from there for you have fulfilled your responsibility (Mt 10:14; Mk 6:11; Lk 9:5). In addition, although the watchman in the Old Testament watch by standing and sounding the trumpet, the one in the New Testament prayed and spoke to those concerned. Jesus himself went to the desert every morning to pray before it was dawn (Mk 1:35) so he can be spiritually charged with God's anointing to warn the Pharisees, Sadducees and Romans. He tells the people to watch and pray so that they can escape the dangers (Lk 21:36).

Jesus then made women watch women too. It is not only men who should watch over the society, but women too must watch. That is why we have watchwomen. There is neither Jew nor Greek, there is neither bond nor free, there is neither male nor female: for ye are all one in Christ Jesus. The status of watchman was extended to women with his death on the Christ of Calvary because all were now baptized by one spirit into one body as we all become the children of God by faith in Christ Jesus (Gal 3:28 , I Cor 12:13, Col 3:11,Gal 3:26, Gal 5:6, 24, Philippians 1:1).

Paul was a great preacher we all know. He sums up some of the places that rejected him as a watchman but reinforces that the rejection of man is not that of God as God delivered him from them all (2 Tim 3:11). When he went to Antioch where Jesus' followers were called Christians for the first time, he preached and many believed. But later, he was rejected, and he shook off the dust of their feet against them and went to Iconium (Acts 13:51). Take the warning to those who want to hear watchman!

Then he went to Macedonia. When they opposed him, he shook his raiment and placed their own blood unto their heads (Acts 18:6). Then he left again and went back to the same Iconium where he has been rejected the first time. This time, after preaching, a great multitude of both Jews and Greeks believed (Acts 14:1). Then when they were rejected the second time, they went to Lystrai, Iconium, and Antioch (Acts 14:1, 19, 21).

Therefore, watchmen and watchwomen must rise up and be counted. Many dress like pastors, but they are fake, actually hirelings siphoning their wealth into their bank accounts. Why have churches increased, yet sin has super increased rather than the opposite. Where are the watchmen and women to warn the victims killed daily by murderers? Where are they? God has made you a watchman and watchwoman. Are you in your post? Are you warning the sinners of the dangers of their sins? Even some watchmen and watchwomen have been taken unawares. Are you taking heed therefore unto yourselves, and to all the flock, over the which the Holy Ghost hath made you overseers, to feed the church of God, which he hath purchased with his own blood?

Until then, are you a watchman or watchwoman?

Chapter Thirty-Seven

Hope in Hopelessness

Brethren,

Only death brings the end of hope. As long as we are alive let us have hope that God does not fail. He may not walk with the pace of a man, but He is never in a hurry and never late. Keep trusting Jesus; he will never fail you. Life always serves us with a plate we did not order. However, let us not worry; we should only know the Cook is our very own Father: Jesus whose meal will bless our hearts.

Fear sometimes cripples us but let faith moves us to higher bounds. Look around you, that is not how you began. You are not what you want to be, but thank God, you are not what you used to be. To every tunnel, there is an end. Our dark days may be long and dreary but stay focus, your ray of light just proves you are winning. You will make it.

There are many in heaven looking down and hoping you make it too. Would you fail them? You owe them the responsibility of making it and seeing Father Abraham, Moses, Joshua, Gideon, Deborah, Esther, Daniel, John the Baptist, Paul, Apollos and finally Jesus.

My Brethren, the days keep getting darker and darker and evil seems enveloping us all. You may be cast down but don't be downcast. Tell them though I am knocked down I am not knocked out. I am still in the ring for it is not who wins but who can put up a fight till the Master comes. Care not how fast the other is running. When you stumble, lift yourself up and keep running; knowing that it is not a race to find the first but one of finishers.

I have made up my mind to leave misery and the world behind me. I take up my full armor to face the tides of life that try to beat me round. At times I crawl with tears in my eyes, other times I run with joy in my heart. I may not be walking and I am not running but know that, in so far as I am not standing I am on the move. Every early morning, I made some phone calls to my friends and Jesus always picks his. More so, He does not complain what time is this. He tells me all the time, coheir, I am on my way, just a little bit of patience.

That at once illumines and brightens my day because while on earth, the sister of IRS loved him as he even paid his taxes from the mouth of a fish. His legs were his car and now that gas prices are hiking, he will be treading on familiar territory. Everywhere he visited, he was doing good. Some people did not need to buy medication for he used just mud to heal their blindness. He prepared a meal in the presence of foes and friends alike and their baskets were overfull in a football field. I mean just with two loaves and five fish he will feed more than ten thousand.

Look at you with teary heart or even face. Why are you silently crying when you can make that early phone call? You think your situation is hopeless and life is not fair. Indeed life is hopeless and unfair without a chemistry with Jesus. Seest thou not that thy Lord lovest thee that much my brethren? Why lookest thou unto thyself when thy Hope beckoneth? Your Master, though gone is always around you. You know, He loves you very much. If the devil tries to push you over you over push him in prayers till you make the Lord your delight. When trials and temptations come over you in their myriads you be the overcomer the Lord has smoothen. Say to yourself, I came to this world, not of my choice but of His own making. I was made more than a conqueror without a vote; I shall live as a conqueror in the midst of warriors and shall die a conqueror even if all others are killed. Lord unto you I surrender my life.

Until then, only dead people lose hope.

Chapter Thirty-Eight

Make The Old Year New

When I was a young preacher I asked one of our area pastors how I could be very effective in any locality. He enumerated three things: don't touch their money, do not seduce their women, and identify yourself with them taking for granted that God is your focus. One proverb says: find out why you failed and you will not fail again. We all had some dark pages in 2007 that we don't want to follow us in 2008. Please, make 2008 new!

Humanity's biggest problem is the attempt to sideline God. In 2008 I have seen cronies and strangers divorce or break up and the theme of predilection: financial differences. Surely you have heard God say: "the LOVE OF MONEY is the root of all evil". If money is too important than human beings then you will not keep a relationship. Another reason that has broken so many relationships is illicit sex: adultery and others. If sex to you is an exercise in futility that you do indiscriminately then you will soon find out that if relationship was only sex then Hollywood would be in a better predicament unfortunately, if love was shoes, then Hollywood would charter all sizes. Our quest for power has also kept us away from those that would have made us happy. People have faked happiness but as you know: plastic surgery may repair a damaged face but a plastic smile will be insufficient for a miserable life. Deep in you, are you really happy?

Dear friends, just like no one wants to be second class or a spare tire show those you meet that they are special in your life and they will stay for long. Everybody wants to be loved, accepted and valued. These are all Bible concepts for they are summarized in the second most important commandment: "love your neighbor as yourself". I have been young, and now am old; yet have I not seen the righteous forsaken, nor his seed begging bread (Ps 37:25). Therefore, "delight thyself also in the LORD; and he shall give thee the desires of thine heart" (Ps 37:4). If you want to be happy, reduce your appetite for money, look at sex as a gift from God to be used properly and show genuine concern for others. In short love God 100% and your neighbor as yourself.

This month I will not post new screeds because I will be reading over my previous posts to correct some of the cosmetic grammatical mistakes I can find. My desire is that my blog will contribute to an extent to the great happiness and peace that eluded you last year. If you are struggling with any addiction, debts, weight or loneliness and you need help please; feel free to write me even anonymously like some do through my email: saintarrey@yahoo.com.

The God we serve neither slumbers nor sleeps. He is never in a hurry but he is never late. He walks with a pace unfamiliar to humans but leaves his footprints everywhere He passes. The only that turns a seabed to a highway. He converts a fish into a submarine, and turns birds into chefs. He performs surgery without spilling blood and his voice is thunder. The saliva of his Son Jesus is an eye drop for the blind to see. The IRS will worship Him because He orders even fishes to pay his taxes on time. In his days, coffin makers had bad business because he usually raised up the dead. As if not enough; he rejected two strikes you are out and installed seventy times seven times before you were out. He walked like a man but spoke as God. Horoscope and tarot readers hated him because he read their minds and foretold the future. Keep trusting in Jesus; He will never fail you.

Until then, God never ever fails!

Chapter Thirty-Nine

Where Are All God's Watchmen and Watchwomen?

Are there still watchmen and watchwomen? Why is the destruction of the family so high? How come people are so alienated from God, addicted to technology, environmentally destructive? Can we explain the invasion of individualism and subsequent loss of community life? Why are there too many slaves to debts and consumerism? The rich ruling the masses ? How come the neglect of children and maltreatment of women and men more common nowadays? Where are the watchmen and watchwomen when the media that was the source of truth now is the corrupt box of lies? Why does this seem the age where there is total neglect of the old and sick? The watchman was to look out against danger, foreign invaders. He was to spy, observe and watch at the city. As the watchmen were never to keep silent about impending danger, those that have been called by the lord to denounce evil and bring people to Christ cannot be silent (Isaiah:62:6-7). The task of the watchman and women nowadays.

So let me ask you this as a Christian who have you warned since you became a Christian. Do you know an adulterer and yet you have stayed mum? Do you know those who are openly living in sin, but you believe that is their lifestyle or alternative lifestyle? Do you know a known drug dealer or anyone who is doing drugs but you have decided to keep quiet because it is not your business? What about the scammer you hang out with? If that person dies, God will hold you accountable. Do you know a preacher who is pilfering from the church and the rich who are stealing from the poor, yet you think it is their problem and not yours? Do you have a father or mother who is a racist, but you refuse to warn them because you think how they want to live their lives is not your business? Hear me and hear me well; God holds you responsible if you know it but do not warn them. Perhaps, this is only the Old Testament. So what does the New Testament say about it too?

There are several passages in the Bible where the Bible is commissioned to preach the gospel to every creature (Mt 28:18-20), but the reaction to the gospel and the reaction of the preachers is what I will discuss here. I will start with the commission to Ezekiel. God tells him to act as a sentinel, warn both the wicked and the righteous. If the wicked abandons his wicked ways and returns unto the Lord, he will be saved, but if he does not, when he dies, his blood will be in his own hands. However, if the sentinel (Ezekiel) does not warn him, when he dies, God will hold Ezekiel responsible. Why was he to warn the righteous too? If verse 24 establishes this "But when the righteous turneth away from his righteousness, and committeth iniquity, *and* doeth according to all the abominations that the wicked *man* doeth, shall he live? All his righteousness that he hath done shall not be mentioned: in his trespass that he hath trespassed, and in his sin that he hath sinned, in them shall he die. " So the assignment here is very precise. Preach and warn the wayward of their waywardness. Whatever they do with that warning is their problem and not yours; you have fulfilled your responsibility. You can hear God through the mouth of Jeremiah rebuking the Isrealites that "Thus saith the LORD, Stand ye in the ways, and see, and ask for the old paths, where *is* the good way, and walk therein, and ye shall find rest for your souls. But they said, We will not walk *therein* (Jeremiah:6:16)."

The first person to overtly repeat such a stand was Jesus. Although John The Baptist practiced it, but he did not preach it. John preached to those who wanted to listen and left those who did not. He even packed and went into the desert to live so that only those who wanted to really listen to him heard him. Simply because you warn people of their evil does not mean they will listen. However, when Jesus came, the story was different. He established three basic truths about the watchman. When you go out to preach, live with someone you know and don't change houses. Preach to those who want to listen and those who do not , leave them alone and go your way. God will take it from there for you have fulfilled your responsibility (Mt 10:14; Mk 6:11; Lk 9:5). In addition, although the watchman in the Old Testament watch by standing and sounding the trumpet, the one in the new Testament prayed and spoke to those concerned. Jesus himself went to the desert every morning to pray before it was dawn (Mk 1:35) so he can be spiritually charged with God's anointing to warn the Pharisees, Sadducees and Romans. He tells the people to watch and pray so that they can escape the dangers (Lk 21:36).

Jesus then made women watch women too. It is not only men who should watch over the society, but women too must watch. That is why we have watchwomen. There is neither Jew nor Greek, there is neither bond nor free, there is neither male nor female: for ye are all one in Christ Jesus. The status of watchman was extended to women with his death on the Christ of Calvary because all were now baptized by one spirit into one body as we all become the children of God by faith in Christ Jesus (Gal 3:28, I Cor 12:13, Col 3:11,Gal 3:26, Gal 5:6, 24, Philippians 1:1).

Paul was a great preacher we all know. He sums up some of the places that rejected him as a watchman but reinforces that the rejection of man is not that of God as God delivered him from them all (2 Tim 3:11). When he went to Antioch where Jesus' followers were called Christians for the first time, he preached and many believed. But later, he was rejected, and he shook off the dust of their feet against them and went to Iconium (Acts 13:51). Take the warning to those who want to hear watchman!

Then he went to Macedonia. When they opposed him, he shook his raiment and placed their own blood unto their heads (Acts 18:6). Then he left again and went back to the same Iconium where he has been rejected the first time. This time, after preaching, a great multitude of both Jews and Greeks believed (Acts 14:1). Then when they were rejected the second time, they went to Lystrai, Iconium, and Antioch (Acts 14:1, 19, 21).

Therefore, watchmen and watchwomen must rise up and be counted. Many dress like pastors, but they are fake, actually hirelings siphoning their wealth into their bank accounts. Why have churches increased, yet sin has super increased rather than the opposite? Where are the watchmen and women to warn the victims killed daily by murderers? Where are they? God has made you a watchman and watchwoman. Are you in your post? Are you warning the sinners of the dangers of their sins? Even some watchmen and watchwomen have been taken unawares. Are you taking heed therefore unto yourselves, and to all the flock, over the which the Holy Ghost hath made you overseers, to feed the church of God, which he hath purchased with his own blood?

Until then, are you a watchman or watchwoman?

INDEXES OF BIBLE QUOTATIONS

Hope In Hopelessness

INDEX OF WORDS

Hope In Hopelessness

(no heading)

Quitters 37
Race 37, 77, 78, 84, 109
Races..............................6, 7
Recommending.................61
Rejection.........2, 3, 107, 115
Relationship 111
Relationships.............11, 111
Righteousness 31, 35, 52, 69, 97, 98, 106, 114
Romans 24, 107, 115
Rome................................22
Salvation 3, 20, 29
Scammers..........................18
Schadenfreude...................78
Shepherd 99, 100, 101
Shepherds........................100
Sin 14, 15, 16, 25, 46, 81, 97, 105, 106, 108, 113, 114, 116
Sing.................37, 53, 59, 86
Sins 10, 15, 16, 31, 46, 49, 52, 69, 75, 97, 108, 116
Slave 68
Society .4, 18, 20, 28, 33, 34, 95, 107, 115
Song............2, 37, 53, 55, 59
Spectators.........................83
Spirit ..22, 23, 24, 27, 35, 42, 44, 57, 71, 91, 92, 99, 107, 115
Spiritually 22, 66, 86, 107, 115
Suicide11, 13, 26, 48, 54, 64, 103
Teach.2, 5, 42, 73, 74, 97, 98

Teacher 11, 40, 51
Temptations 4, 27, 64, 85, 110
Testimony 91
True friend 9
Trustworthy................40, 44
Truth ..40, 49, 74, 75, 76, 94, 105, 113
Tunnel......................83, 109
TV................................1, 61
US ...11, 22, 24, 41, 100, 102
Useless..............1, 74, 86, 90
Vow....20, 23, 79, 80, 81, 82, 87, 88, 89
Vows...............10, 69, 80, 89
War 27, 44, 58, 81, 87, 95
Warfare 86, 100
Warriors..............85, 88, 110
Watch...5, 43, 44, 49, 55, 64, 95, 105, 107, 113, 115
Watchman......105, 107, 108, 113, 115, 116
Watchmen......105, 108, 113, 116
Watchwoman 108, 116
Watchwomen .105, 107, 108, 113, 115, 116
Wishes.................30, 81, 99
Womb 33
Wombs.............................34
Workman 74, 75, 76
Wrath 46
Zion 53, 59

INDEX OF NAMES

Hope In Hopelessness